Editorial project:
© 2023 booq publishing, S.L.
c/ Domènech, 7-9, 2º 1ª
08012 Barcelona, Spain
T: +34 93 268 80 88
www.booqpublishing.com

ISBN 978-84-9936-657-9 [EN]
ISBN 978-84-9936-648-7 [DE]

monsa
publications

© 2023 Instituto Monsa de ediciones, S.L.
c/ Gravina, 43
08930 Sant Adrià de Besós, Barcelona, Spain
T: +34 93 381 00 93
www.monsa.com
monsa@monsa.com

ISBN: 978-84-17557-63-8

Editorial coordinator:
Claudia Martínez Alonso

Art director:
Mireia Casanovas Soley

Editor:
Daniela Santos Quartino

Layout:
Cristina Simó Perales

Translation:
© booq publishing, S.L.

Printing in Spain

6   INTRODUCTION

8   BASIC PROJECTS

20   BOSC ARCHITECTES

34   BREWIN DESIGN OFFICE

46   CARME PARDO
     ARQUITECTURA INTERIOR

58   CLO STUDIOS

70   CO-LAB DESIGN OFFICE

84   DA BUREAU

96   D'AUSSY INTERIORS

108 FAR STUDIO

122 GOLANY ARCHITECTS

136 I-IN

148 JESSICA BATAILLE
     THE LIFESTYLE COMPANY

162 MARLENE ULDSCHMIDT STUDIO

174 NC DESIGN & ARCHITECTURE

188 ODELIA BARZILAY
     INTERIOR DESIGN

200 STUDIO RAZAVI ARCHITECTURE

214 STUDIO STOOKS

226 ZOZAYA ARQUITECTOS

Slow interiors transcend trends to generate environments in tune with the values of those who live in them. They are designs that lead to calm and enjoyment of the passing of time. These environments, which invite us to take a more leisurely approach, are the immediate response to the frenetic lifestyle that prevails today.

The trend has been brewing for some time, with the resurgence of minimalism, or the reappraisal of Japanese wabi sabi. But it is since the Covid pandemic that it has crept more forcefully into the work of interior designers – and the social networks – as a declaration of intent: happiness is not a goal, but a journey, which one chooses to undertake every day. Enjoyment is in the process, in the moments - small or large - that shape the journey.

Slow living is about living consciously, appreciating the environment and turning to nature. Translated into residential and commercial design, they are spaces oriented towards sustainability, but not only. They have a preference for local products, rescue tradition and incorporate artisan know-how.

Slow environments prioritise light, seek out textures and use noble materials such as wood, raffia, cotton, linen, plaster and stone. Designers invest in handcrafted aesthetics and unique pieces of furniture because the aim is not only to transmit calm, but to create atmospheres that last over time. This is why this movement emphasises the process behind it, not just what the finished product looks like.

The projects presented in this book assume these pillars, each one in its own style and open with each page, the doors to enjoyment.

Slow Interiors gehen über Trends hinaus und schaffen Umgebungen, die mit den Werten der Menschen, die in ihnen leben, in Einklang stehen. Es sind Entwürfe, die zu Ruhe und Freude am Vergehen der Zeit führen. Diese Umgebungen, die uns zu einer gemächlicheren Herangehensweise einladen, sind die unmittelbare Antwort auf den hektischen Lebensstil, der heute vorherrscht.

Der Trend zeichnet sich schon seit einiger Zeit ab, mit dem Wiederaufleben des Minimalismus oder der Neubewertung des japanischen wabi sabi. Doch seit der Covid-Pandemie hat er sich stärker in die Arbeit von Innenarchitekten - und in die sozialen Netzwerke – als Absichtserklärung eingeschlichen: Glück ist kein Ziel, sondern eine Reise, die man jeden Tag aufs Neue beschreitet. Das Vergnügen liegt im Prozess, in den kleinen und großen Momenten, die die Reise prägen.

Slow Living bedeutet, bewusst zu leben, die Umwelt zu schätzen und sich der Natur zuzuwenden. Übertragen auf die Gestaltung von Wohn- und Geschäftsräumen handelt es sich um Räume, die auf Nachhaltigkeit ausgerichtet sind, aber nicht nur. Sie bevorzugen lokale Produkte, retten die Tradition und lassen handwerkliches Know-how einfließen.

Langsame Umgebungen bevorzugen Licht, suchen nach Texturen und verwenden edle Materialien wie Holz, Bast, Baumwolle, Leinen, Gips und Stein. Die Designer investieren in handgefertigte Ästhetik und einzigartige Möbelstücke, denn sie wollen nicht nur Ruhe vermitteln, sondern auch eine Atmosphäre schaffen, die lange anhält. Deshalb betont diese Bewegung den Prozess, der dahinter steht, und nicht nur, wie das fertige Produkt aussieht.

Die in diesem Buch vorgestellten Projekte gehen von diesen Säulen aus, jede auf ihre eigene Art und Weise, und öffnen mit jeder Seite die Türen zum Vergnügen.

Les intérieurs lents transcendent les tendances pour créer des environnements en phase avec les valeurs de ceux qui les habitent. Ce sont des conceptions qui conduisent au calme et à la jouissance du temps qui passe. Ces environnements, qui nous invitent à une approche plus ludique, sont la réponse immédiate au mode de vie frénétique qui prévaut aujourd'hui.

La tendance se dessine depuis un certain temps, avec la résurgence du minimalisme, ou la revalorisation du wabi sabi japonais. Mais c'est depuis la pandémie de Covid qu'elle s'est insinuée avec plus de force dans le travail des architectes d'intérieur - et sur les réseaux sociaux - comme une déclaration d'intention : le bonheur n'est pas un but, mais un voyage, que l'on choisit d'entreprendre chaque jour. Le plaisir est dans le processus, dans les moments - petits ou grands - qui façonnent le voyage.

Le slow living consiste à vivre consciemment, à apprécier l'environnement et à se tourner vers la nature. Traduits en design résidentiel et commercial, ce sont des espaces orientés vers la durabilité, mais pas seulement. Ils ont une préférence pour les produits locaux, sauvent la tradition et intègrent le savoir-faire artisanal.

Les environnements lents privilégient la lumière, recherchent les textures et utilisent des matériaux nobles comme le bois, le raphia, le coton, le lin, le plâtre et la pierre. Les designers investissent dans une esthétique artisanale et des meubles uniques, car l'objectif est non seulement de transmettre le calme, mais aussi de créer des atmosphères qui durent dans le temps. C'est pourquoi ce mouvement met l'accent sur le processus qui le sous-tend, et pas seulement sur l'aspect du produit fini.

Les projets présentés dans ce livre assument ces piliers, chacun dans son propre style et ouvrent, à chaque page, les portes du plaisir.

Los interiores *slow* trascienden tendencias para generar ambientes a tono con los valores de quienes los habitan. Son diseños que conducen a la calma y al disfrute del devenir del tiempo. Estos ambientes que invitan a asumir una perspectiva más pausada, son la respuesta inmediata al estilo de vida frenético que predomina en la actualidad.

La tendencia viene gestándose desde hace tiempo, con el resurgimiento del minimalismo, o la reapreciación del *wabi sabi* japonés. Pero es a partir de la pandemia del Covid que se cuela más contundentemente en el trabajo de los interioristas —y las redes sociales— como toda una declaración de intenciones: la felicidad no es un objetivo, sino un viaje, que se elige emprender cada día. El disfrute está en proceso, los momentos —pequeños o grandes— que dan forma al camino.

El slow living es vivir con consciencia, apreciar el entorno y recurrir a la naturaleza. Traducido al diseño residencial y comercial, son espacios orientados a la sostenibilidad, aunque no solamente. Tienen preferencia por los productos locales, rescatan la tradición e incorporan el saber hacer artesanal.

Los ambientes slow priorizan la luz, buscan los juegos de texturas y recurren a materiales nobles como la madera, la rafia, el algodón, el lino, el yeso y la piedra. Los diseñadores invierten en estéticas artesanales y piezas de mobiliario único porque el objetivo no solo es transmitir calma, sino crear ambientes que perduren en el tiempo. Por ello este movimiento pone el acento en el proceso que hay detrás, no sólo el aspecto que tiene el producto acabado.

Los proyectos que se presentan en este libro, asumen estos pilares, cada uno en su estilo y abren con cada página, las puertas para disfrutar.

BASIC PROJECTS

BEN TOWILL - KATE TOWILL

Basic Projects is a lifestyle-driven design and development firm founded by Ben & Kate Towill in 2015. Basic Projects' offices are based in Charleston, SC, and together the team work closely to make spaces that are not only beautiful but functional and comfortable too. With over 15 years in the design and hospitality industry, the team behind Basic Projects offer a uniquely intentional approach to design, how it lives and the purpose it serves through the everyday. The Basic Projects portfolio ranges from residential and hospitality design services to self-propelled development projects and in-house operations for a number of restaurants and boutique hotels in the Southeastern U.S.

Basic Projects ist ein Design- und Entwicklungsunternehmen, das von Ben und Kate Towill im Jahr 2015 gegründet wurde. Die Büros des Studios befinden sich in Charleston, South Carolina, und das Team arbeitet daran, Räume zu schaffen, die nicht nur schön, sondern auch funktional und komfortabel sind. Mit über 15 Jahren Erfahrung in der Design- und Gastgewerbebranche bietet das Team hinter Basic Projects einen bewussten Ansatz für Design, wie es gelebt wird und welchen Zweck es im Alltag erfüllt. Das Portfolio von Basic Projects reicht von Designdienstleistungen für Wohn- und Gastgewerbe bis hin zu eigenen Entwicklungsprojekten und dem Betrieb mehrerer Restaurants und Boutique-Hotels im Südosten der Vereinigten Staaten.

Basic Projects est une société de conception et de développement, fondée par Ben et Kate Towill en 2015. Les bureaux du studio sont situés à Charleston, en Caroline du Sud, et son équipe travaille à la création d'espaces qui ne sont pas seulement beaux, mais aussi fonctionnels et confortables. Avec plus de 15 ans d'expérience dans le secteur du design et de l'hôtellerie, l'équipe derrière Basic Projects propose une approche intentionnelle du design, de la manière dont il est vécu et de l'objectif qu'il sert au quotidien. Le portefeuille de Basic Projects s'étend des services de conception résidentielle et hôtelière aux projets de développement interne et aux opérations internes pour plusieurs restaurants et hôtels-boutiques dans le sud-est des États-Unis.

Basic Projects es una empresa de diseño y desarrollo, fundada por Ben y Kate Towill en 2015. Las oficinas de la firma se encuentran en Charleston, Carolina del Sur, y cuenta con un equipo que trabaja para crear espacios que no solo sean hermosos, sino también funcionales y cómodos. Con más de 15 años en la industria del diseño y la hostelería, el equipo detrás de Basic Projects ofrece un enfoque intencional al diseño, cómo se vive, y el propósito al que sirve a través de lo cotidiano. La cartera de Basic Projects abarca desde servicios de diseño residencial y de hostelería hasta proyectos de desarrollo propios y operaciones internas para varios restaurantes y hoteles boutique en el sureste de Estados Unidos.

POE AVENUE

SULLIVAN'S ISLAND, SOUTH CAROLINA, UNITED STATES
Photos: © Olivia Rae James

The design of this home is inspired by the homeowners' surfing trips to Fiji and Hawaii, and their Californian blood. The exterior of the house is reminiscent of French Polynesia. In the interiors, however, raw materials such as concrete, plaster, linen, brass and white oak transport us to the image of the California coast, where light reigns and where less is more.

The kitchen cabinets are in white oak with plaster frames and contrast with the warm grey concrete worktop, a combination that is repeated in the main washbasin. The lacquered bar counter has a custom handmade tile back panel by London-based Smink Things.

The double-sided plaster fireplace creates two atmospheres and maintains a sense of spaciousness. The oak dining table sits on vintage flat-weave rugs purchased on trips. In the living room, the wooden coffee table and linen sofas accompany the artwork commissioned from renowned artist and surfer Ty Williams. The collection of wall lamps was designed by Workstead, who also created the leather chair in the kitchen. The mix of vintage and modern, characteristic of Basic Projects, dominates the character of the rooms.

La conception de cette maison s'inspire des voyages de surf des propriétaires à Fidji et à Hawaï, ainsi que de leur sang californien. L'extérieur de la maison rappelle la Polynésie française. Dans les intérieurs, en revanche, les matériaux bruts tels que le béton, le plâtre, le lin, le laiton et le chêne blanc nous transportent à l'image de la côte californienne, où la lumière règne et où le moins est le plus.

Les armoires de cuisine sont en chêne blanc avec des cadres en plâtre et contrastent avec le plan de travail en béton gris chaud, une combinaison que l'on retrouve dans le lavabo principal. Le comptoir de bar laqué est doté d'un panneau arrière en carrelage fait main par la société londonienne Smink Things.

La cheminée en plâtre à double face crée deux atmosphères et maintient un sentiment d'espace. La table à manger en chêne repose sur des tapis vintage à tissage plat achetés en voyage. Dans le salon, la table basse en bois et les canapés en lin accompagnent l'œuvre d'art commandée à l'artiste et surfeur renommé Ty Williams. La collection d'appliques a été conçue par Workstead, qui a également créé le fauteuil en cuir dans la cuisine. Le mélange de vintage et de moderne, caractéristique de Basic Projects, domine le caractère des chambres.

Das Design dieses Hauses ist inspiriert von den Surftrips der Hausbesitzer nach Fidschi und Hawaii sowie von ihrem kalifornischen Blut. Das Äußere des Hauses erinnert an Französisch-Polynesien. In den Innenräumen hingegen versetzen uns rohe Materialien wie Beton, Gips, Leinen, Messing und Weißeiche in das Bild der kalifornischen Küste, wo das Licht regiert und weniger mehr ist.

Die Küchenschränke sind aus weißer Eiche mit Gipsrahmen und kontrastieren mit der warmen grauen Betonarbeitsplatte, eine Kombination, die sich im Hauptwaschtisch wiederholt. Der lackierte Bartresen ist mit einer handgefertigten Kachelrückwand des Londoner Unternehmens Smink Things versehen.

Der doppelseitige Gipskamin schafft zwei Atmosphären und sorgt für ein Gefühl von Großzügigkeit. Der Esstisch aus Eichenholz steht auf alten, auf Reisen gekauften Flachgewebeteppichen. Im Wohnzimmer werden der hölzerne Couchtisch und die Leinensofas von einem Kunstwerk begleitet, das der bekannte Künstler und Surfer Ty Williams in Auftrag gegeben hat. Die Wandleuchtenkollektion wurde von Workstead entworfen, die auch den Lederstuhl in der Küche entworfen haben. Die für Basic Projects charakteristische Mischung aus Vintage und Moderne prägt den Charakter der Räume.

El diseño en esta vivienda se inspira en los viajes de los propietarios surfistas a las islas Fiyi y Hawai, y su sangre californiana. El exterior de la casa recuerda a la Polinesia Francesa. Sin embargo en los interiores, los materiales en bruto como el hormigón, el yeso, el lino, el latón y el roble blanco, traen la imagen de la costa de California, donde impera la luz y el menos es más.

Los armarios de la cocina son de roble blanco con marcos de yeso y contrastan con la encimera de hormigón teñida de gris cálido, una combinación que se repite en el lavabo principal. La barra de bar lacada, tiene un panel trasero de azulejos hechos a mano y personalizados de la firma londinense Smink Things.

La chimenea de yeso de doble cara genera dos ambientes y mantiene una sensación de amplitud. La mesa de roble del comedor se apoya sobre alfombras vintage de tejido plano adquiridas en viajes. En el salón, la mesa de centro de madera y los sofás de lino acompañan a la obra de arte encargada al conocido artista y surfista Ty Williams. La colección de lámparas de pared ha sido diseñada por Workstead, que también creó la silla de cuero de la cocina. La mezcla entre lo vintage y lo moderno, característica de Basic Projects, domina el carácter de las habitaciones.

BOSC ARCHITECTES

bosc-architectes.com

BOSC ARCHITECTES

JEAN BOSC - ARTHUR BOSC

Forerunner of an experimental return to traditional techniques, architect Hugues Bosc, founded an agency in Saint Rémy in 1973, with a vision that has led to the revival of vernacular construction in French Provence. In 2013, Jean and Arthur Bosc took over the agency to create Bosc Architectes. Jean Bosc trained at the Julian ESAG Met Academy in Penninghen and at the Paris Belleville School of Architecture, and Arthur has a degree in engineering from the INP in Grenoble and graduated from the Ecole Nationale Supérieure d'Architecture in Marseille. Today, the management team is a duo that complements each other perfectly and exudes a joyful and creative energy.

Der Architekt Hugues Bosc, Vorreiter einer experimentellen Rückbesinnung auf traditionelle Techniken, gründete 1973 in Saint Rémy ein Büro mit einer Vision, die zu einer Wiederbelebung der traditionellen Bauweise in der französischen Provence führte. Im Jahr 2013 übernahmen Jean und Arthur Bosc das Büro und gründeten Bosc Architectes. Jean Bosc hat eine Ausbildung an der Julian ESAG Met Academy in Penninghen und an der Pariser Architekturschule Belleville absolviert, während Arthur einen Abschluss als Ingenieur am INP in Grenoble und einen Abschluss an der Ecole Nationale Supérieure d'Architecture in Marseille hat. Heute ist das Führungsteam ein Duo, das sich perfekt ergänzt und eine fröhliche und kreative Energie ausstrahlt.

Précurseur d'un retour expérimental aux techniques traditionnelles, l'architecte Hugues Bosc, a fondé une agence à Saint Rémy en 1973, avec une vision qui a conduit au renouveau de la construction vernaculaire en Provence française. En 2013, Jean et Arthur Bosc ont repris l'agence pour créer Bosc Architectes. Jean Bosc a été formé à l'Académie Julian ESAG Met de Penninghen et à l'école d'architecture de Paris Belleville. Arthur est ingénieur diplômé de l'INP de Grenoble et diplômé de l'Ecole Nationale Supérieure d'Architecture de Marseille. Aujourd'hui, l'équipe de direction est un duet qui se complète parfaitement et dégage une énergie joyeuse et créative.

Precursor de un retorno experimental a las técnicas tradicionales, el arquitecto Hugues Bosc, fundó una agencia en Saint Rémy en 1973, con una visión que ha propiciado el renacimiento de la construcción vernácula en la provenza francesa. En 2013, Jean y Arthur Bosc, retoman la agencia para crear Bosc Architectes. Jean Bosc se formó en la Academia Julian ESAG Met de Penninghen y en la Escuela de Arquitectura de París Belleville, y Arthur, es licenciado en ingeniería en el INP de Grenoble y graduado de la Escuela Nacional Superior de Arquitectura de Marsella. En la actualidad, el equipo directivo forma un dúo que se complementa perfectamente y desprende una gran energía alegre y creativa.

LA FENIÈRE DANS LES ALPILLES MAISON

SAINT ÉTIENNE-DU-GRÈS, PROVENCE - ALPES-CÔTE D'AZUR, FRANCE

Photos: © Herve Hote

This dwelling was originally a labyrinth of small, dark rooms. Situated in a forest in the south of France, the architects saw its enormous potential and set about renovating it in the spirit of freedom and simplicity inherent in Mediterranean holiday homes.

To gain space and natural light they re-organised the internal layout. They knocked down walls and relocated the rooms following a logical and fluid connection. They worked from a sculptural point of view so that curves, lines, objects, lights, passages and angles generated interesting compositions.

In addition to the architectural solutions, this effect was also sought with the materials and colours. For the surfaces, they opted for Zellige terracotta tiles handmade in Morocco and Bejmat tiles, which allowed them to create a variety of patterns. The floor is also the result of natural and varnished Bejmats laid in a herringbone pattern. The wooden furniture and craftsman-inspired pieces stand out against the almost bare walls. To reinforce the flow, shelving and benches were used in selected areas of the house.

Cette demeure de était à l'origine un labyrinthe de petites pièces sombres. Située dans une forêt du sud de la France, les architectes ont vu son énorme potentiel et ont entrepris de la rénover dans l'esprit de liberté et de simplicité inhérent aux maisons de vacances méditerranéennes.

Pour gagner de l'espace et de la lumière naturelle, ils ont réorganisé l'aménagement intérieur. Ils ont abattu des murs et déplacé les pièces en suivant une connexion logique et fluide. Ils ont travaillé d'un point de vue sculptural, de sorte que les courbes, les lignes, les objets, les lumières, les passages et les angles ont généré des compositions intéressantes.

Outre les solutions architecturales, cet effet a également été recherché au niveau des matériaux et des couleurs. Pour les surfaces, ils ont opté pour des carreaux de terre cuite Zellige fabriqués à la main au Maroc et des carreaux Bejmat, ce qui leur a permis de créer une variété de motifs. Le sol est également le résultat de Bejmats naturels et vernis posés en chevrons. Les meubles en bois et les pièces d'inspiration artisanale se détachent sur les murs presque nus. Pour renforcer le flux, des étagères et des bancs ont été utilisés dans certaines zones de la maison.

Dieses Haus war ursprünglich ein Labyrinth aus kleinen, dunklen Räumen. In einem Wald in Südfrankreich gelegen, erkannten die Architekten das enorme Potenzial des Hauses und machten sich daran, es im Geiste der Freiheit und Schlichtheit der mediterranen Ferienhäuser zu renovieren.

Um Platz und natürliches Licht zu gewinnen, wurde die Innenaufteilung neu organisiert. Sie rissen Wände ein und verlegten die Räume nach einer logischen und fließenden Verbindung. Sie arbeiteten nach bildhauerischen Gesichtspunkten, so dass Kurven, Linien, Objekte, Lichter, Durchgänge und Winkel interessante Kompositionen ergaben.

Neben den architektonischen Lösungen wurde diese Wirkung auch mit den Materialien und Farben angestrebt. Für die Oberflächen entschieden sie sich für in Marokko handgefertigte Zellige-Terrakottafliesen und Bejmat-Fliesen, mit denen sie eine Vielzahl von Mustern gestalten konnten. Der Boden ist ebenfalls das Ergebnis von natürlichen und lackierten Bejmats, die in einem Fischgrätenmuster verlegt sind. Die Holzmöbel und handwerklich inspirierten Stücke heben sich von den fast kahlen Wänden ab. Um den Fluss zu verstärken, wurden in ausgewählten Bereichen des Hauses Regale und Bänke eingesetzt.

Esta vivienda era originalmente un laberinto de habitaciones pequeñas y oscuras. Situada en un bosque en el sur de Francia, los arquitectos vieron su enorme potencial y se plantearon reformarla con el espíritu de libertad y sencillez inherente a las casas de vacaciones mediterráneas.

Para ganar espacio y luz natural reorganizaron la distribución interna. Derribaron muros y reubicaron las estancias siguiendo una conexión lógica y fluida. Se trabajó con un pnto de vista escultórico para que las curvas, las líneas, los objetos, las luces, los pasajes y los ángulos generen composiciones interesantes

Además de las soluciones arquitectónicas, se buscó ese efecto también con los materiales y las tonalidades. Para las superficies se decantaron por azulejos de terracota Zellige fabricados a mano en Marruecos, y baldosas Bejmat, que les permitieron crear variedad de patrones. El suelo también es resultado de un revestimiento a base de Bejmats naturales y barnizados colocados en forma de espiga. Los muebles de madera y las piezas de inspiración artesana resaltan frente a las paredes casi desnudas. Para reforzar la fluidez, se apostó por estanterías y bancos de obra en espacios seleccionados de la casa.

Sketch site plan

Ground floor plan

First floor plan

1. Entry
2. Living room
3. Kitchen
4. Bathroom
5. Corridor
6. Bedroom

BREWIN DESIGN OFFICE

ROBERT CHENG

At Brewin Design Office, creativity is born of authenticity and affection, and is reflected in an artisanal approach to the creation of furniture and spaces, a perceptible passion for design and respect for the identity of each project. Working in different scales and genres has allowed for constant experimentation, with an overall ambition to achieve a sense of beauty governed by order, rhythm and detail. Since Robert Cheng founded the studio in 2012, this direction has remained steadfast. Cheng is an architect and interior designer. His philosophy is influenced by his knowledge and sensitivity to diverse cultures, the result of his extensive travels in Asia, America and Europe.

Bei Brewin Design Office entsteht Kreativität aus Authentizität und Zuneigung und spiegelt sich in einer handwerklichen Herangehensweise an die Gestaltung von Möbeln und Räumen, einer spürbaren Leidenschaft für Design und dem Respekt vor der Identität eines jeden Projekts wider. Die Arbeit in verschiedenen Maßstäben und Genres ermöglichte ein ständiges Experimentieren mit dem Ziel, einen Sinn für Schönheit zu erreichen, der von Ordnung, Rhythmus und Details bestimmt wird. Seit der Gründung des Studios durch Robert Cheng im Jahr 2012 ist diese Richtung ungebrochen. Cheng ist Architekt und Innenarchitekt. Seine Philosophie ist geprägt von seinem Wissen und seiner Sensibilität für verschiedene Kulturen, die er auf seinen ausgedehnten Reisen in Asien, Amerika und Europa erworben hat.

Chez Brewin Design Office, la créativité naît de l'authenticité et de l'affection, et se traduit par une approche artisanale de la création de meubles et d'espaces, une passion perceptible pour le design et le respect de l'identité de chaque projet. Travailler à différentes échelles et dans différents genres a permis une expérimentation constante, avec l'ambition générale d'atteindre un sens de la beauté régi par l'ordre, le rythme et le détail. Depuis que Robert Cheng a fondé le studio en 2012, cette orientation est restée inébranlable. Cheng est architecte et décorateur d'intérieur. Sa philosophie est influencée par ses connaissances et sa sensibilité à l'égard de diverses cultures, fruit de ses nombreux voyages en Asie, en Amérique et en Europe.

En Brewin Design Office, la creatividad nace de la autenticidad y el afecto, y se refleja en un enfoque artesanal hacia la creación de muebles y espacios, una pasión perceptible por el diseño y el respeto por la identidad de cada proyecto. Trabajar a distintas escalas y géneros le ha permitido una experimentación constante, con la ambición general de alcanzar una sensación de belleza regida por el orden, el ritmo y el detalle. Desde que Robert Cheng fundó el estudio en 2012, esta dirección se ha mantenido firme. Cheng es arquitecto y diseñador de interiores. Su filosofía está influenciada por sus conocimientos y sensibilidades hacia diversas culturas, fruto de sus extensos viajes por Asia, América y Europa.

THE GREEN APARTMENT

SINGAPORE

Photos: © Khoo Guo Jie

The Green Apartment is a private residence located in a luxury low density residential development in Singapore. The project consisted of an extensive renovation inspired by the lush gardens visible from the balcony. There was a total reconfiguration of the apartment's layout for efficiency and an improved experience.

In a newly designed entry foyer, a private lift vestibule opens into a dramatic gallery of sculptural green solid onyx pillars that act as a screen between the arrival space and the main common areas. In the living and dining rooms, textural richness continues and is seen on lightly silvered-stucco walls and ceilings, custom designed furniture and carpentry, all of which are paired with the adept curation of carefully sourced old and new pieces.

The living room has a spatial generosity stemming from the lofty 3.5 m ceilings. This is further enhanced by abundant natural light entering from the 9 m long balcony that accentuates the subtle silvery glimmer of the ivory stucco wall.

The indoor white oak flooring visually merges with the natural bleached teak floors at the balcony, where an existing sunken pool was levelled to increase the usable space of the terrace. On the balcony walls, terracotta tiles add depth and a traditional handcrafted touch.

The Green Apartment est une résidence privée située dans un lotissement de luxe à Singapour. Le projet consistait en une rénovation inspirée des jardins luxuriants visibles depuis le balcon. L'agencement de l'appartement a été reconfiguré en faveur de l'efficacité et d'une expérience améliorée.

Le nouveau hall d'entrée est un espace privé avec ascenseur qui s'ouvre sur une galerie spectaculaire de piliers en onyx vert massif, servant d'écran aux zones communes. Dans le salon et la salle à manger, la richesse des textures se retrouve dans les murs et les plafonds en stuc, les meubles sur mesure et les boiseries, le tout associé à une sélection de pièces anciennes et nouvelles.

Le salon a une générosité spatiale dérivée des hauts plafonds de 3,5 mètres. L'abondante lumière naturelle qui entre par le balcon de neuf mètres de long accentue le subtil éclat argenté du mur en stuc ivoire. Le sol intérieur en chêne blanc s'harmonise visuellement avec le sol en teck blanchi naturel du balcon, où se trouve une piscine. Sur les murs du balcon, les carreaux en terre cuite ajoutent de la profondeur et une touche d'artisanat traditionnel.

Dans tout le reste de la maison, le bois de hickory occupe une place centrale. Associés à des tons neutres et à des tissus naturels dans les chambres, ils créent une atmosphère équilibrée et calme dans tous les espaces, qui dégagent une qualité masculine et zen. Avec l'utilisation du marbre Calacatta Gold dans toutes les salles de bains, l'élément de grand luxe dans l'appartement s'étend d'un bout à l'autre.

The Green Apartment ist ein privates Wohnhaus in einer Luxuswohnanlage in Singapur. Das Projekt bestand aus einer Renovierung, die von den üppigen Gärten inspiriert war, die man vom Balkon aus sehen konnte. Der Grundriss der Wohnung wurde zugunsten von Effizienz und einem besseren Erlebnis umgestaltet.

Die neue Lobby ist ein privater Raum mit Aufzug, der sich zu einer dramatischen Galerie aus massiven grünen Onyxsäulen öffnet, die als Abschirmung zu den Gemeinschaftsbereichen dient. Im Wohn- und Esszimmer findet sich der Reichtum der Texturen in den Stuckwänden und -decken, den maßgefertigten Möbeln und Holzarbeiten, die mit einer Auswahl an antiken und neuen Stücken kombiniert sind.

Das Wohnzimmer hat eine räumliche Großzügigkeit, die von den hohen 3,5 Meter hohen Decken herrührt. Das reichlich vorhandene natürliche Licht, das durch den neun Meter langen Balkon einfällt, betont den subtilen Silberglanz der elfenbeinfarbenen Stuckwand. Der Innenboden aus weißer Eiche harmoniert optisch mit dem natürlichen, gebleichten Teakholzboden des Balkons, auf dem sich ein Swimmingpool befindet. An den Wänden des Balkons sorgen Terrakottafliesen für Tiefe und einen Hauch von traditioneller Handwerkskunst.

Im gesamten Haus steht das Hickoryholz im Mittelpunkt. In Kombination mit neutralen Tönen und natürlichen Stoffen in den Schlafzimmern wird eine ausgewogene und ruhige Atmosphäre in allen Räumen geschaffen, die eine maskuline, zenartige Qualität ausstrahlen. Die Verwendung von Calacatta-Gold-Marmor in allen Bädern verleiht der Wohnung einen Hauch von Luxus.

The Green Apartment es una residencia privada en una urbanización de lujo en Singapur. El proyecto consistió en una renovación inspirada en los exuberantes jardines visibles desde el balcón. La distribución del apartamento se reconfiguró a favor de la eficiencia y una experiencia mejorada.

El nuevo vestíbulo es un espacio privado con ascensor que se abre a una espectacular galería de pilares de ónice verde macizo, y que actúa como pantalla con las zonas comunes. En el salón y el comedor, la riqueza de texturas se aprecia en las paredes y los techos de estuco, los muebles a medida y la carpintería, todo ello combinado con una selección de piezas antiguas y nuevas.

El salón tiene una generosidad espacial derivada de los altos techos de 3,5 metros. La abundante luz natural que entra por el balcón de nueve metros de largo acentúa el sutil brillo plateado de la pared de estuco marfil. El suelo interior de roble blanco se funde visualmente con el suelo natural de teca blanqueada del balcón, donde se encuentra una piscina. En las paredes del balcón, las baldosas de terracota añaden profundidad y un toque artesanal tradicional.

En el resto de la casa, la madera de nogal americano es protagonista. Combinada con tonos neutros y tejidos naturales en los dormitorios, se consigue un ambiente equilibrado y tranquilo en todos los espacios, que desprenden una cualidad masculina y zen. Con el uso de mármol Calacatta Gold en todos los cuartos de baño, el elemento de alto lujo en 39 el apartamento se extiende de extremo a extremo.

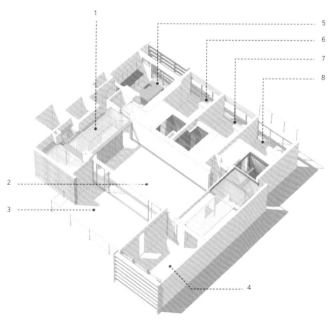

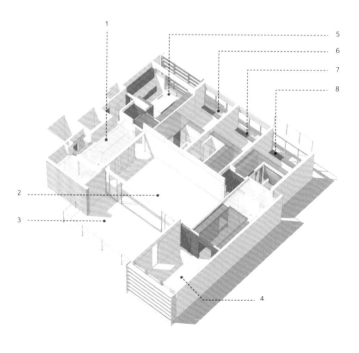

Material diagram

1. Entrance hall
2. Dining/living room
3. Terrace
4. Master bedroom

5. Kitchen
6. Study
7. Bedroom 2
8. Bedroom 3

- Stone 1
- Stone 2
- Timber

CARME PARDO ARQUITECTURA INTERIOR

CARME PARDO

Carme Pardo trained at the Escuela Superior de Diseño de Interiores EIADE in Barcelona. After creating her first studio specialising in textiles, where she discovered the importance of textures and working with natural and neutral materials, she began her professional career in 2008. As an interior designer she has carried out projects in Spain and the south of France. Her works are mainly residential, although in recent years she has also ventured into the field of small charming hotels. "I like functional interiors without excesses, which form part of the context and the architecture, working with shapes and light, explains the designer. We seek to create balanced and timeless spaces, tailor-made suits for each client".

Carme Pardo absolvierte ihre Ausbildung an der Escuela Superior de Diseño de Interiores EIADE in Barcelona. Nach der Gründung ihres ersten auf Textilien spezialisierten Studios, in dem sie die Bedeutung von Texturen und die Arbeit mit natürlichen und neutralen Materialien entdeckte, begann sie 2008 ihre berufliche Laufbahn. Als Innenarchitektin hat sie Projekte in Spanien und Südfrankreich verwirklicht. Ihre Arbeiten sind vor allem im Wohnbereich angesiedelt, obwohl sie sich in den letzten Jahren auch in den Bereich der kleinen charmanten Hotels vorgewagt hat. „Ich mag funktionale Innenräume ohne Übertreibungen, die sich in den Kontext und die Architektur einfügen und mit Formen und Licht arbeiten, erklärt der Designer, wir versuchen, ausgewogene und zeitlose Räume zu schaffen, die für jeden Kunden maßgeschneidert sind".

Carme Pardo a suivi une formation à l'Escuela Superior de Diseño de Interiores EIADE de Barcelone. Après avoir créé son premier atelier spécialisé dans le textile, où elle a découvert l'importance des textures et du travail avec des matériaux naturels et neutres, elle a commencé sa carrière professionnelle en 2008. En tant qu'architecte d'intérieur, elle a réalisé des projets en Espagne et dans le sud de la France. Ses travaux sont principalement résidentiels, bien que ces dernières années, elle se soit également aventurée dans le domaine des petits hôtels de charme. «J'aime les intérieurs fonctionnels sans excès, qui s'intègrent au contexte et à l'architecture, en travaillant les formes et la lumière, explique le designer. Nous cherchons à créer des espaces équilibrés et intemporels, des costumes sur mesure pour chaque client.»

Carme Pardo se formó en la Escuela Superior de Diseño de Interiores EIADE de Barcelona. Después de crear su primer estudio especializado en textiles, donde descubrió la importancia de las texturas y de trabajar con materiales naturales y neutros, en 2008 inició su trayectoria profesional. Como diseñadora de interiores ha realizado proyectos en España y el sur de Francia. Sus trabajos son principalmente residenciales, aunque en los últimos años también ha incursionado en el campo de los pequeños hoteles con encanto. «Me gustan los interiores funcionales y sin excesos, que formen parte del contexto y de la arquitectura, trabajando con las formas y la luz —explica la diseñadora— Buscamos crear espacios equilibrados y atemporales, trajes a medida para cada cliente».

LE PAVILLON

ALMIÈRES, LA LOZÈRE, FRANCE

Photos: © Eugeni Pons

This contemporary design pavilion, which seems to be suspended over the breathtaking Tarn Gorges, is the refuge that the couple commissioned the owners to build to escape from the city and live in a calm and serene environment, close to their venture project, the Almières Retreat, where they organise yoga and wellness retreats.

Its strategic location provides a unique experience of intimate contact with nature and total disconnection.

To reinforce this feeling, the choice of materials was key. On the outside, the combination of local wood in the latticework and stone on the walls blends in with the rocky mountain. Inside, natural oak wood in different finishes covers the ceilings, floors and walls, creating an extension of the interior to the exterior.

The designer combined traditional materials such as black zimbawe granite in the kitchen with natural textures such as linen and wool in the curtains, creating an elegant atmosphere of warmth and comfort, even in sub-zero temperatures in winter, thanks to the suspended fireplace in the living room. Simplicity in the design of the spaces and furnishings, as well as carefully considered lighting, contribute to creating a minimalist and calm interior, "a haven for the soul".

Ce pavillon au design contemporain, qui semble suspendu au-dessus des époustouflantes Gorges du Tarn, est le refuge que le couple a fait construire pour s'échapper de la ville et vivre dans un environnement calme et serein, à proximité de leur projet d'entreprise, la Retraite des Almières, où ils organisent des retraites de yoga et de bien-être.

Son emplacement stratégique offre une expérience unique de contact intime avec la nature et de déconnexion totale.

Pour renforcer ce sentiment, le choix des matériaux était essentiel. À l'extérieur, la combinaison de bois local dans les treillis et de pierre sur les murs s'harmonise avec la montagne rocheuse. À l'intérieur, du bois de chêne naturel de différentes finitions recouvre les plafonds, les sols et les murs, créant ainsi une extension de l'intérieur vers l'extérieur.

Le designer a combiné des matériaux traditionnels tels que le granit noir zimbawe dans la cuisine avec des textures naturelles comme le lin et la laine dans les rideaux, créant ainsi une atmosphère élégante, chaleureuse et confortable, même par des températures négatives en hiver, grâce à la cheminée suspendue dans le salon. La simplicité de la conception des espaces et du mobilier, ainsi qu'un éclairage soigneusement étudié, contribuent à créer un intérieur minimaliste et calme, « un havre pour l'âme ».

Dieser zeitgenössische Design-Pavillon, der über der atemberaubenden Gorges du Tarn zu schweben scheint, ist das Refugium, das das Ehepaar den Eigentümern in Auftrag gegeben hat, um der Stadt zu entfliehen und in einer ruhigen und gelassenen Umgebung zu leben, in der Nähe ihres Projekts, dem Almières Retreat, wo sie Yoga- und Wellness-Retreats veranstalten.

Seine strategische Lage bietet eine einzigartige Erfahrung des intimen Kontakts mit der Natur und der totalen Abgeschiedenheit.

Um dieses Gefühl zu verstärken, war die Wahl der Materialien entscheidend. Von außen fügt sich die Kombination aus einheimischem Holz im Fachwerk und Stein an den Wänden in die felsige Bergwelt ein. Im Inneren sind Decken, Böden und Wände mit natürlichem Eichenholz in verschiedenen Ausführungen verkleidet, so dass sich der Innenraum nach außen hin verlängert.

Der Designer kombinierte traditionelle Materialien wie schwarzen Zimbawe-Granit in der Küche mit natürlichen Texturen wie Leinen und Wolle in den Vorhängen und schuf so eine elegante Atmosphäre der Wärme und Behaglichkeit, selbst bei Minusgraden im Winter, dank des hängenden Kamins im Wohnzimmer. Die schlichte Gestaltung der Räume und des Mobiliars sowie die durchdachte Beleuchtung tragen dazu bei, ein minimalistisches und ruhiges Interieur zu schaffen, „eine Oase für die Seele".

Éste pabellón de diseño contemporáneo que parece estar suspendido sobre las impresionantes Gargantas del Tarn, es el refugio que encargaron construir la pareja de propietarias para huir de la ciudad y vivir en un entorno de calma y serenidad, cerca de su proyecto de emprendimiento, el Almières Retreat, donde organizan retiros de yoga y bienestar.

Su estratégica ubicación proporciona una experiencia singular de íntimo contacto con la naturaleza y de desconexión total.

Para reforzar ese sentimiento, la selección de los materiales fue clave. En el exterior la combinación de la madera autóctona en las celosías y la piedra en las paredes se confunden con la montaña rocosa. En el interior, la madera de roble natural en distintos acabados, reviste techos, suelos y paredes, creando una prolongación del interior hacía el exterior.

La diseñadora combinó materiales tradicionales como el granito negro zimbawe en la cocina, con texturas naturales como el lino, o la lana en las cortinas, creando una atmósfera elegante de calidez y confort, incluso con temperaturas bajo cero en el invierno, gracias a la chimenea suspendida en el salón. La simplicidad en el diseño de los espacios y del mobiliario, así como una estudiada iluminación contribuye a crear un interior minimalista y calmo, «un refugio para el alma».

CLO STUDIOS

CHLOE TOZER

CLO Studios was conceived by mother and daughter designers Trudy and Chloe Tozer. Combining Trudy's extensive interior design experience, and Chloe's established background in Fine Art and Jewellery, a multi-disciplinary partnership was forged between the two. Chloe's innate curiosity and fearless, intuitive approach to design is the foundation of the firm. Inspiration is drawn from the world's rich and vibrant cultures, from which she weaves her artistic narratives with each client's desires. Her aim is to create spaces to be admired through work that is based on research and careful design resulting in luxury residential interiors and bespoke commercial spaces.

CLO Studios wurde von den Designerinnen Trudy und Chloe Tozer, Mutter und Tochter, gegründet. Durch die Kombination von Trudys umfassender Erfahrung in der Innenarchitektur und Chloes fundiertem Hintergrund in den Bereichen Kunst und Schmuck wurde eine multidisziplinäre Partnerschaft zwischen den beiden geschmiedet. Chloes angeborene Neugier und ihre furchtlose, intuitive Herangehensweise an das Design sind die Grundlage des Unternehmens. Ihre Inspiration schöpft sie aus den reichen und lebendigen Kulturen der Welt, aus denen sie ihre künstlerischen Erzählungen mit den Wünschen ihrer Kunden verwebt. Ihr Ziel ist es, durch ihre Arbeit, die auf Forschung und sorgfältigem Design basiert, Räume zu schaffen, die bewundert werden können, und so luxuriöse Wohnräume und maßgeschneiderte Geschäftsräume zu schaffen.

CLO Studios a été conçu par les designers mère et fille Trudy et Chloe Tozer. En combinant la vaste expérience de Trudy dans le domaine de la décoration d'intérieur et l'expérience de Chloé dans le domaine des beaux-arts et de la bijouterie, un partenariat multidisciplinaire s'est formé entre les deux. La curiosité innée de Chloé et son approche intrépide et intuitive du design constituent le fondement de l'entreprise. Elle puise son inspiration dans les cultures riches et vibrantes du monde, à partir desquelles elle tisse ses récits artistiques en fonction des désirs de chaque client. Son objectif est de créer des espaces qui suscitent l'admiration grâce à un travail basé sur la recherche et une conception soignée, qui se traduit par des intérieurs résidentiels de luxe et des espaces commerciaux sur mesure.

CLO Studios fue concebido por las diseñadoras Trudy y Chloe Tozer, madre e hija. Combinando la amplia experiencia en diseño de interiores de Trudy, y la consolidada formación de Chloe en Bellas Artes y Joyería, se forjó una asociación multidisciplinar entre ambas. La curiosidad innata y el enfoque valiente e intuitivo de Chloe hacia el diseño son la base de la firma. La inspiración son las diferentes culturas del mundo, ricas y vibrantes, de las cuales entrelaza sus narrativas artísticas con los deseos de cada cliente. Su objetivo es crear espacios para ser admirados y su trabajo, se basa en la investigación en profundidad y el diseño cuidadoso que resulta en interiores residenciales de lujo y comerciales a medida.

SKY GARDEN

NOOSA HEADS, QUEENSLAND, AUSTRALIA

Photos: © David Chatfield

CLO Studios provided the interior decoration for this project by building designers Chris Clout Design, located in the exclusive area of Noosa Queensland. Taking a counterpoint to the home's very defined exteriors, a neutral and soothing palette was created for the interiors. With the use of natural Australian timbers, and the choice of serene colours taken from the environment, the house gained warmth.

A detail that is unique to this house was applied to each space in Sky Garden, such as the custom-designed furniture. The 4.5 m long dining table is made from blackbutt wood, with logs hand milled by a local craftsman. At the entrance, a stunning 3D artwork commissioned from local artist Stacy Madden (Woven Husk) stands out. The piece is paired with a cowhide rug by Kyle Bunting.

The pool area represents the owners' desire for a colourful and fun area. The key was to create a space that was not distinct from the interior, but an extension of the design with a playful twist. Circular staircases are rare, but always a charming way to break up the straight lines and draw the eye to the sky and the sun on the terrace.

CLO Studios a assuré la décoration intérieure de ce projet des desinateurs de bâtiments Chris Clout Design, situé dans la zone exclusive de Noosa Queensland. En contrepoint des extérieurs très définis de la maison, une palette neutre et apaisante a été créée pour les intérieurs. Avec l'utilisation de bois naturel australien et le choix de couleurs sereines tirées de l'environnement, la maison a gagné en chaleur.

Un détail qui est unique à cette maison a été appliqué à chaque espace de Sky Garden, comme le mobilier conçu sur mesure. La table à manger de 4,5 m de long est fabriquée en bois de blackbutt, dont les rondins sont fraisés à la main par un artisan local. À l'entrée, une étonnante œuvre d'art en 3D commandée à l'artiste locale Stacy Madden (Woven Husk) se détache. La pièce est associée à un tapis en peau de vache de Kyle Bunting.

L'espace piscine représente le désir des propriétaires d'avoir un espace coloré et amusant. La clé était de créer un espace qui ne soit pas distinct de l'intérieur, mais une extension du design avec une touche ludique. Les escaliers circulaires sont rares, mais ils constituent toujours un moyen charmant de rompre les lignes droites et d'attirer le regard vers le ciel et le soleil de la terrasse.

CLO Studios lieferte das Innendesign für dieses Projekt des bauplaner Chris Clout Design, das in der exklusiven Gegend von Noosa Queensland liegt. Als Kontrapunkt zu den scharf umrissenen Außenbereichen des Hauses wurde für die Innenräume eine neutrale und beruhigende Farbpalette geschaffen. Durch die Verwendung natürlicher australischer Hölzer und die Wahl ruhiger, der Umgebung entnommener Farben erhielt das Haus eine warme Ausstrahlung.

Ein für dieses Haus einzigartiges Detail wurde in jedem Raum von Sky Garden angewandt, wie z. B. die speziell entworfenen Möbel. Der 4,5 m lange Esstisch ist aus Schwarzbutt-Holz gefertigt, dessen Stämme von einem örtlichen Handwerker handgefräst wurden. Am Eingang sticht ein beeindruckendes 3D-Kunstwerk ins Auge, das bei der lokalen Künstlerin Stacy Madden (Woven Husk) in Auftrag gegeben wurde. Das Stück wird mit einem Kuhfellteppich von Kyle Bunting kombiniert.

Der Poolbereich entspricht dem Wunsch der Eigentümer nach einem farbenfrohen und unterhaltsamen Bereich. Der Schlüssel war, einen Raum zu schaffen, der sich nicht von der Inneneinrichtung unterscheidet, sondern eine Erweiterung des Designs mit einer spielerischen Note ist. Rundtreppen sind selten, aber immer eine reizvolle Möglichkeit, die geraden Linien aufzubrechen und den Blick auf den Himmel und die Sonne auf der Terrasse zu lenken.

CLO Studios se encargó de la decoración en este proyecto de los proyectistas Chris Clout Design, situado en la exclusiva zona de Noosa Queensland. Tomando como contrapunto los exteriores muy definidos de la vivienda, se creó una paleta neutra y relajante para los interiores. Con el uso de maderas naturales australianas, y la elección de colores serenos tomados del entorno, la casa ganó calidez.

En cada espacio de Sky Garden se aplicó un detalle que es exclusivo para esta casa, como los muebles diseñados a medida. La mesa del comedor de 4,5 metros de largo está hecha con madera de blackbutt, y troncos fresados a mano por un artesano local. En la entrada, destaca una impresionante obra de arte en 3D encargada al artista local Stacy Madden (Woven Husk). La pieza combina con una alfombra de piel de vaca de Kyle Bunting.

El área de la piscina representa la voluntad de los propietarios de contar con una zona colorida y divertida. La clave era crear un espacio que no se diferenciara del interior, sino que fuera una extensión del diseño con un toque lúdico. Las escaleras circulares son poco frecuentes, pero siempre son una manera encantadora de romper las líneas rectas y atraer la mirada hacia el cielo y el sol en su terraza.

CO-LAB DESIGN OFFICE

JOANA GOMES - JOSHUA BECK

Founded by Joana Gomes and Joshua Beck in 2010, CO-LAB DESIGN OFFICE is an architecture, design and construction studio based in Tulum, Mexico. Inspired by the natural beauty of Yucatan, their projects foster a deep connection with the natural world. Their work embraces sustainable principles, prioritising the use of locally sourced natural materials and handcrafted finishes. The aesthetic tends towards a certain raw minimalism mitigated by the use of landscaping and organic, handcrafted finishes. The office is part design studio and part workshop where objects, furniture and accessories are prototyped, and techniques and materials are experimented with. CO-LAB works directly with artisans to create naturally beautiful environments in harmony with their surroundings.

Das 2010 von Joana Gomes und Joshua Beck gegründete CO-LAB DESIGN OFFICE ist ein Architektur-, Design- und Konstruktionsbüro mit Sitz in Tulum, Mexiko. Inspiriert von der natürlichen Schönheit Yucatans, fördern ihre Projekte eine tiefe Verbundenheit mit der natürlichen Welt. Sie arbeiten nach nachhaltigen Grundsätzen und verwenden vorrangig natürliche Materialien aus der Region und handgefertigte Oberflächen. Die Ästhetik tendiert zu einem gewissen rohen Minimalismus, der durch die Verwendung von Landschaftsgestaltung und organischen, handgefertigten Oberflächen gemildert wird. Das Büro ist zum Teil Designstudio und zum Teil Werkstatt, in der Objekte, Möbel und Accessoires als Prototypen entwickelt und mit Techniken und Materialien experimentiert wird. CO-LAB arbeitet direkt mit Kunsthandwerkern zusammen, um natürlich schöne Umgebungen in Harmonie mit ihrer Umgebung zu schaffen.

Fondé par Joana Gomes et Joshua Beck en 2010, CO-LAB DESIGN OFFICE est un studio d'architecture, de design et de construction basé à Tulum, au Mexique. Inspirés par la beauté naturelle du Yucatan, leurs projets favorisent un lien profond avec le monde naturel. Leur travail s'appuie sur des principes durables, privilégiant l'utilisation de matériaux naturels d'origine locale et de finitions artisanales. L'esthétique tend vers un certain minimalisme brut atténué par l'utilisation de l'aménagement paysager et de finitions organiques et artisanales. Le bureau est à la fois un studio de design et un atelier où des objets, des meubles et des accessoires sont prototypés, et où des techniques et des matériaux sont expérimentés. CO-LAB travaille directement avec les artisans pour créer des environnements naturellement beaux en harmonie avec leur environnement.

Fundado por Joana Gomes y Joshua Beck en 2010, CO-LAB DESIGN OFFICE es un estudio de arquitectura, diseño y construcción con sede en Tulum, México. Inspirados en la belleza natural de Yucatán, sus proyectos fomentan una profunda conexión con el mundo natural. Su trabajo adopta principios sostenibles, prioriza el uso de materiales naturales de origen local y los acabados artesanales. La estética tiende hacia cierto minimalismo crudo mitigado por el uso del paisajismo y los acabados orgánicos y artesanales. La oficina es parte estudio de diseño y parte taller en el que se prototipan objetos, muebles y accesorios, y se experimenta con técnicas y materiales. CO-LAB trabaja directamente con artesanos para crear entornos naturalmente bellos en armonía con su entorno.

CASA AVIV

TULUM, MEXICO

Photos: © César Bejar

Just a stone's throw from Tulum beach and crystal-clear cenotes, this house hides discreetly in the jungle, opening to the outside to create a haven of tranquillity. Composed of two parallel volumes, the house has four en-suite bedrooms, all with views of the jungle. The master bedroom has direct access to the swimming pool and private patio. The living-dining room and kitchen share a double-height space that extends out to the pool and garden through the floor-to-ceiling pivoting glass doors. The result is an integrated environment, full of natural light and visually connected to the garden. The house is oriented from east to west, taking advantage of the winds coming from the coast to achieve cross ventilation.

The finishes and materials used have been handcrafted. The warm grey polished cement walls contrast with the black terrazzo floors. Charred cedar woodwork complements a neutral colour palette. Furniture and light fittings were custom-designed and sourced or manufactured locally. The solid appearance of the house reflects the durability and low maintenance needs of a rental property in a tropical climate.

À deux pas de la plage de Tulum et des cénotes aux eaux cristallines, cette maison se cache discrètement dans la jungle, s'ouvrant sur l'extérieur pour créer un havre de tranquillité. Composée de deux volumes parallèles, la maison dispose de quatre chambres en-suite, toutes avec vue sur la jungle. La chambre principale a un accès direct à la piscine et au patio privé.

Le salon-salle à manger et la cuisine partagent un espace à double hauteur qui s'étend vers la piscine et le jardin à travers les portes vitrées pivotantes du sol au plafond. Le résultat est un environnement intégré, plein de lumière naturelle et visuellement connecté au jardin. La maison est orientée d'est en ouest, profitant des vents venant de la côte pour obtenir une ventilation croisée.

Les finitions et les matériaux utilisés ont été réalisés de manière artisanale. Les murs en ciment poli gris chaud contrastent avec les sols en terrazzo noir. Les boiseries en cèdre carbonisé complètent une palette de couleurs neutres. Les meubles et les luminaires ont été conçus sur mesure et achetés ou fabriqués localement. L'apparence solide de la maison reflète la durabilité et les besoins d'entretien réduits d'une propriété locative dans un climat tropical.

Nur einen Steinwurf vom Strand von Tulum und den kristallklaren Cenoten entfernt, versteckt sich dieses Haus diskret im Dschungel und öffnet sich nach außen, um eine Oase der Ruhe zu schaffen. Das Haus besteht aus zwei parallelen Volumen und hat vier Schlafzimmer mit eigenem Bad, alle mit Blick auf den Dschungel. Das Hauptschlafzimmer hat direkten Zugang zum Swimmingpool und zur privaten Terrasse.

Das Wohn-Esszimmer und die Küche teilen sich einen Raum mit doppelter Höhe, der sich durch die bodentiefen Glasschwingtüren zum Pool und Garten hin öffnet. Das Ergebnis ist eine integrierte Umgebung voller natürlichem Licht und mit einer visuellen Verbindung zum Garten. Das Haus ist von Osten nach Westen ausgerichtet, um die von der Küste kommenden Winde für eine Querlüftung zu nutzen.

Die verwendeten Oberflächen und Materialien sind handgefertigt. Die warmen grauen, polierten Zementwände stehen im Kontrast zu den schwarzen Terrazzoböden. Gekohlte Zedernholzarbeiten ergänzen eine neutrale Farbpalette. Möbel und Beleuchtungskörper wurden individuell entworfen und vor Ort beschafft oder hergestellt. Das solide Erscheinungsbild des Hauses spiegelt die Langlebigkeit und den geringen Wartungsbedarf eines Mietobjekts in einem tropischen Klima wider.

A tan solo un paso de la playa de Tulum y de los cristalinos cenotes, esta casa se esconde discretamente en la jungla, abriéndose al exterior para crear un reductos de tranquilidad. Compuesta por dos volúmenes paralelos, la vivienda cuenta con cuatro habitaciones, todas con vistas a la jungla, y baño. La habitación principal tiene acceso directo a la piscina y patio privado

La sala-comedor y cocina comparten un espacio a doble altura que se extiende hacia la piscina y el jardín a través de las puertas de vidrio pivotantes, de piso a techo. Como resultado se genera un ambiente integrado, lleno de luz natural y conectado visualmente al jardín. La casa está orientada de este a oeste, aprovechando los vientos que llegan desde la costa para lograr así una ventilación cruzada.

Los acabados y materiales utilizados han sido producidos artesanalmente. Los muros de cemento pulido gris cálido, contrastan con los suelos de terrazo negro. La carpintería en madera de cedro carbonizada complementa la paleta neutra. Los muebles y luminarias se diseñaron a medida y se obtuvieron o fabricaron localmente. Eel aspecto solido de la casa refleja las necesidades de durabilidad y bajo mantenimiento de una propiedad de alquiler en un clima tropical.

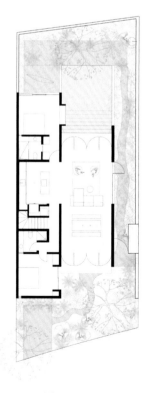

Ground floor plan

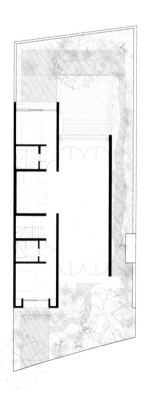

First floor plan

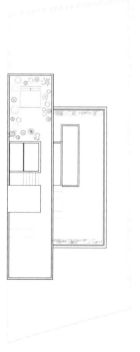

Roof plan

DA BUREAU

BORIS LVOVSKY - ANNA LVOVSKAYA - FEDOR GOREGLYAD - MARIA ROMANOVA

Da Bureau is a team of young architects based in St. Petersburg and Tallinn with the motto "we create interior architecture". The firm has won a number of international awards, including the "Rising Star" award for its founder Boris Lvovsky in Interior Design Magazine's Best of Year in the United States. It has also been on AD Russia magazine's list of the top 100 designers and architects and among the five finalists of the Architizer A+ Awards in the young interior design firm category. He regularly participates in the British Restaurant and Bar Design Awards. His projects are identified by a contemporary, minimalist style and a functionality-oriented approach.

Da Bureau ist ein Team junger Architekten mit Sitz in St. Petersburg und Tallinn und dem Motto „Wir schaffen Innenarchitektur". Das Unternehmen hat eine Reihe von internationalen Auszeichnungen erhalten, darunter die Auszeichnung „Rising Star" für seinen Gründer Boris Lvovsky im Rahmen des Interior Design Magazine's Best of Year in den Vereinigten Staaten. Darüber hinaus wurde es von der Zeitschrift AD Russia in die Liste der 100 besten Designer und Architekten aufgenommen und gehörte zu den fünf Finalisten der Architizer A+ Awards in der Kategorie junge Innenarchitekturbüros. Er nimmt regelmäßig an den British Restaurant and Bar Design Awards teil. Seine Projekte zeichnen sich durch einen zeitgenössischen, minimalistischen Stil und einen funktionsorientierten Ansatz aus.

Da Bureau est une équipe de jeunes architectes basée à Saint-Pétersbourg et à Tallinn qui adopte la devise «nous créons de l'architecture intérieure». Le cabinet a remporté un certain nombre de prix internationaux, notamment le prix «Rising Star» pour son fondateur Boris Lvovsky dans le cadre du concours «Best of Year» de l'Interior Design Magazine aux États-Unis. Elle a également figuré sur la liste des 100 meilleurs designers et architectes du magazine AD Russia et parmi les cinq finalistes des Architizer A+ Awards dans la catégorie des jeunes entreprises de design d'intérieur. Il participe régulièrement aux British Restaurant and Bar Design Awards. Ses projets se caractérisent par un style contemporain et minimaliste et une approche axée sur la fonctionnalité.

Da Bureau es un equipo de jóvenes arquitectos con sede en San Petersburgo y Tallin que se acoge al lema "creamos arquitectura interior". La firma cuenta con un gran número de galardones internacionales, entre ellos el de "Estrella Emergente" de su fundador Boris Lvovsky, en el Best of Year de Interior Design Magazine, en Estados Unidos. También ha estado en la lista de los 100 mejores diseñadores y arquitectos de la revista AD Russia y entre los cinco finalistas de Architizer A+ Awards en la categoría de firma joven de interiorismo. Participa regularmente en los British Restaurant and Bar Design Awards. Sus proyectos se caracterizan por un estilo contemporáneo y minimalista, y un enfoque orientado a la funcionalidad.

OSTERIA BETULLA

SAINT PETERSBURG, RUSSIA

Photos: © Sergey Melnikov

Osteria Betulla is a restaurant by the talented chef, Arslan Berdi. The gastronomic proposal is Italian cuisine, simple and with very high quality products. The design concept of the space is that of a modern Italian canteen with references to the classic. The image resembles an uncluttered, light-filled chapel. The interior has the characteristics of the architectural dramaturgy of traditional churches.

The furnishings refer to Catholic aesthetics. The centre piece of the first room is a metaphorical altar: a large work table for the cook who is in charge of the pasta, with all the tables turned towards him. The highlight of the second room are the church pews in the centre and three icon boxes with the Holy Trinity of Italian cuisine: wine, olive oil and thyme. The drinking troughs common in Italian cities take the form of a wine cooler in the living room and a sink in the bathrooms. The designers' aim was to create a very clean and minimalist look, with as little expressiveness as possible. That is why they used only three basic materials: travertine marble, which is often found in Italian street pavements; wood for the furniture and panelling; and light-coloured plaster as the main material for the walls.

Osteria Betulla est un restaurant du talentueux chef Arslan Berdi. La proposition gastronomique est une cuisine italienne, simple et avec des produits de très haute qualité. Le concept de l'espace est celui d'une cantine italienne moderne avec des références au classique. L'image ressemble à une chapelle épurée et lumineuse. L'intérieur présente les caractéristiques de la dramaturgie architecturale des églises traditionnelles.

L'ameublement fait référence à l'esthétique catholique. La pièce maîtresse de la première salle est un autel métaphorique : une grande table de travail pour le cuisinier qui s'occupe des pâtes, avec toutes les tables tournées vers lui. Le clou de la deuxième pièce est constitué par les bancs d'église au centre et trois boîtes d'icônes avec la Sainte Trinité de la cuisine italienne : vin, huile d'olive et thym. Les abreuvoirs courants dans les villes italiennes prennent la forme d'un refroidisseur de vin dans le salon et d'un évier dans les salles de bains. L'objectif des concepteurs était de créer un look très épuré et minimaliste, avec le moins d'expressivité possible. Ils n'ont donc utilisé que trois matériaux de base : le marbre travertin, que l'on trouve couramment sur les trottoirs italiens, le bois pour les meubles et les lambris, et le plâtre clair comme matériau principal des murs.

Osteria Betulla ist ein Restaurant des talentierten Küchenchefs Arslan Berdi. Das gastronomische Angebot ist italienische Küche, einfach und mit sehr hochwertigen Produkten. Das Designkonzept des Raums ist das einer modernen italienischen Kantine mit Bezügen zur Klassik. Das Bild ähnelt einer unaufgeräumten, lichtdurchfluteten Kapelle. Der Innenraum weist die Merkmale der architektonischen Dramaturgie der traditionellen Kirchen auf.

Das Mobiliar verweist auf die katholische Ästhetik. Das Herzstück des ersten Raums ist ein metaphorischer Altar: ein großer Arbeitstisch für den Koch, der für die Pasta zuständig ist, und alle Tische sind ihm zugewandt. Das Highlight des zweiten Raums sind die Kirchenbänke in der Mitte und drei Ikonenkästen mit der Heiligen Dreifaltigkeit der italienischen Küche: Wein, Olivenöl und Thymian. Die in italienischen Städten üblichen Tränken haben die Form eines Weinkühlers im Wohnzimmer und eines Waschbeckens in den Badezimmern.

Das Ziel der Designer war es, ein sehr klares und minimalistisches Aussehen zu schaffen, mit so wenig Ausdrucksmöglichkeiten wie möglich. Deshalb wurden nur drei grundlegende Materialien verwendet: Travertinmarmor, der häufig in italienischen Straßenpflastern zu finden ist, Holz für die Möbel und die Vertäfelung sowie heller Putz als Hauptmaterial für die Wände.

Osteria Betulla es un restaurante del talentoso chef, Arslan Berdi. La propuesta gastronómica es de cocina italiana, sencilla y con productos de muy alta calidad. El concepto de diseño del espacio, es el de una cantina italiana moderna con referencias a lo clásico. La imagen se asemeja a una capilla despejada y llena de luz. El interior tiene las características de la dramaturgia arquitectónica de las iglesias tradicionales.

El mobiliario hace referencia a la estética católica. La pieza central de la primera sala es un altar metafórico: una gran mesa de trabajo para el cocinero que se encarga de la pasta, con todas las mesas giradas hacia él. El punto fuerte de la segunda sala son los bancos de iglesia en el centro y tres cajas de iconos con la Santísima Trinidad de la cocina italiana: el vino, el aceite de oliva y el tomillo. Los bebederos habituales en las ciudades italianas por su parte, adoptaron la forma de enfriador de vino en la sala, y de lavabo en los baños.

El objetivo de los diseñadores fue crear un aspecto muy pulcro y minimalista, con la menor expresividad posible. Por eso utilizaron solo tres materiales básicos: el travertino, que suele encontrarse en los pavimentos de las calles italianas; madera para los muebles y paneles, y yeso de color claro como material principal en las paredes.

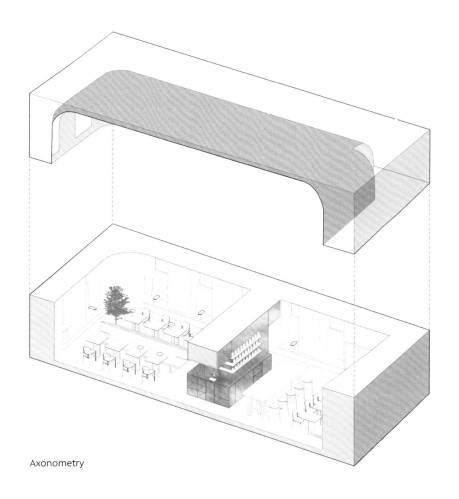

Axonometry

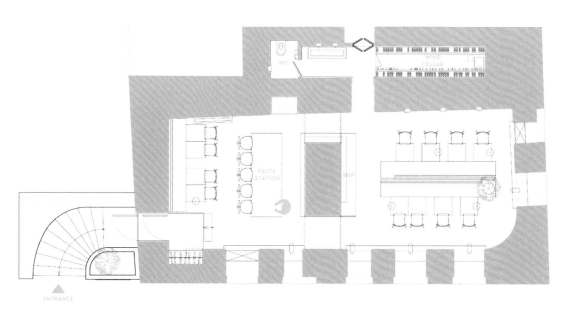

Floor plan

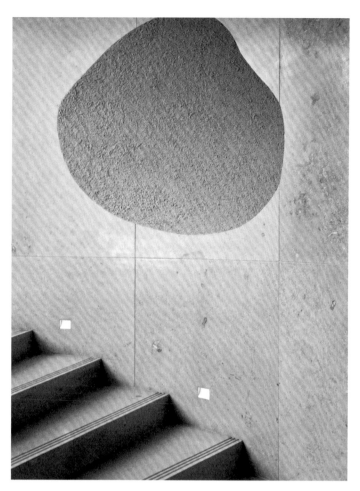

D'AUSSY INTERIORS

CLARA JOLY D'AUSSY

With a long international experience in the interior design sector, Clara Joly d'Aussy runs the studio she founded in 2017 with her father Dominique Joly d'Aussy, in Alt Empordà (Spain). The designer has collaborated with renowned architecture and interior design studios in Australia, such as Alexander and Co and the Japanese Koichi Takada, on residential and restoration projects. On her return to Barcelona, she settled in the Empordà, a region in Catalonia framed by the Mediterranean and the Pyrenees. Her second homes and new construction projects are focused on the Mediterranean style and the Catalan essence, integrating the environment and materials of the region.

Clara Joly d'Aussy verfügt über eine langjährige internationale Erfahrung im Bereich der Innenarchitektur und leitet das Studio, das sie 2017 zusammen mit ihrem Vater Dominique Joly d'Aussy in Alt Empordà (Spanien) gegründet hat. Der Designer hat mit renommierten Architektur- und Innenarchitekturbüros in Australien wie Alexander and Co und dem Japaner Koichi Takada an Wohn- und Restaurierungsprojekten zusammengearbeitet. Nach ihrer Rückkehr nach Barcelona ließ sie sich im Empordà nieder, einer Region in Katalonien, die vom Mittelmeer und den Pyrenäen eingerahmt wird. Seine Zweitwohnungen und Neubauprojekte sind auf den mediterranen Stil und das katalanische Wesen ausgerichtet und integrieren die Umgebung und die Materialien der Region.

Forte d'une longue expérience internationale dans le secteur de la décoration intérieure, Clara Joly d'Aussy dirige le studio qu'elle a fondé en 2017 avec son père Dominique Joly d'Aussy, dans l'Alt Empordà (Espagne). Le designer a collaboré avec des studios d'architecture et de décoration intérieure renommés en Australie, comme Alexander and Co et le Japonais Koichi Takada, sur des projets résidentiels et de restauration. De retour à Barcelone, elle s'installe dans l'Empordà, une région de Catalogne encadrée par la Méditerranée et les Pyrénées. Ses résidences secondaires et ses projets de construction neuve sont axés sur le style méditerranéen et l'essence catalane, en intégrant l'environnement et les matériaux de la région.

Con una larga experiencia internacional en el sector del interiorismo, Clara Joly d'Aussy dirige el estudio que fundó en el año 2017 con su padre Dominique Joly d'Aussy, en el Alt Empordà (España). La diseñadora ha colaborado con reputados estudios de arquitectura y diseño de interiores en Australia, como Alexander and Co y el japonés Koichi Takada, en proyectos residenciales y de restauración. A su regreso a Barcelona, se instaló en el Empordà, una región en Cataluña enmarcada por el Mediterráneo y los Pirineos. Sus proyectos de segundas residencias y obra nueva están enfocados al estilo mediterráneo y a la esencia catalana, integrando el entorno y los materiales de la región.

LLAFRANC

GIRONA, SPAIN

Photos: © Stella Rotger (Revista *El Mueble*) | Styling: Olga Gilbernet

The design of this new-build house on the Costa Brava responds to the request of a family looking for a country and beach house that would allow them to disconnect from the hectic pace of modern life. The contemporary architecture of the building by architect Damián Ribas was the canvas on which Clara Joly d'Aussy set out to give the house warmth by bringing the Mediterranean and the greenery of the Empordà into the interior.

To achieve this, she used wood in furniture and cladding, natural fibers such as rattan, jute and esparto grass, and beige and earth tones. One of the biggest challenges was to separate the kitchen, dining room and living room. To filter the light and divide these spaces without closing them off, the interior designer used vertical sliding doors made of wooden slats. The same slats, but horizontally, complete the cupboards and interior doors, giving the house continuity. The porch was completely integrated with the interior thanks to a metal and reed pergola, and the white fabric curtains that match the gentle sea breeze.

The lighting has been another key aesthetic element: industrial lamps mixed with rattan and other paper lamps create a warm atmosphere which, combined with the wood, create a spirit of pure holiday relaxation. The signature furniture was made by local craftsmen using reused materials, or simply customised for the project.

Der Entwurf dieses Neubaus an der Costa Brava entspricht dem Wunsch einer Familie, die ein Haus auf dem Land und am Strand suchte, um von der Hektik des modernen Lebens abschalten zu können. Die zeitgenössische Architektur des Gebäudes des Architekten Damián Ribas war die Leinwand, auf der Clara Joly d'Aussy dem Haus Wärme verleihen wollte, indem sie das Mittelmeer und das Grün des Empordà in das Innere brachte.

Um dies zu erreichen, verwendete sie Holz für Möbel und Verkleidungen, Naturfasern wie Rattan, Jute und Espartogras sowie Beige- und Erdtöne. Eine der größten Herausforderungen bestand darin, Küche, Esszimmer und Wohnzimmer voneinander zu trennen. Um das Licht zu filtern und die Räume zu unterteilen, ohne sie zu verschließen, verwendete der Innenarchitekt vertikale Schiebetüren aus Holzlamellen. Die gleichen Latten, jedoch horizontal, vervollständigen die Schränke und Innentüren und verleihen dem Haus Kontinuität. Die Veranda wurde dank einer Pergola aus Metall und Schilf und den weißen Stoffvorhängen, die zur sanften Meeresbrise passen, vollständig in den Innenraum integriert.

Die Beleuchtung ist ein weiteres ästhetisches Schlüsselelement: Industrielampen, gemischt mit Rattan- und anderen Papierlampen, schaffen eine warme Atmosphäre, die in Verbindung mit dem Holz ein Gefühl von purer Urlaubsentspannung erzeugt. Die charakteristischen Möbel wurden von lokalen Handwerkern aus wiederverwendeten Materialien hergestellt oder einfach für das Projekt angepasst.

La conception de cette maison de construction neuve sur la Costa Brava répond à la demande d'une famille qui recherchait une maison de campagne et de plage qui leur permettrait de se déconnecter du rythme effréné de la vie moderne. L'architecture contemporaine du bâtiment de l'architecte Damian Ribas a été la toile sur laquelle Clara Joly d'Aussy a entrepris de donner de la chaleur à la maison en faisant entrer la Méditerranée et la verdure de l'Empordà à l'intérieur.

Pour ce faire, elle a utilisé le bois dans les meubles et les revêtements, des fibres naturelles telles que le rotin, le jute et l'alfa, ainsi que des tons beiges et terreux. L'un des plus grands défis était de séparer la cuisine, la salle à manger et le salon. Pour filtrer la lumière et diviser ces espaces sans les fermer, l'architecte d'intérieur a utilisé des portes coulissantes verticales en lattes de bois. Les mêmes lattes, mais horizontalement, complètent les armoires et les portes intérieures, donnant ainsi une continuité à la maison. Le porche a été complètement intégré à l'intérieur grâce à une pergola en métal et roseau, et aux rideaux en tissu blanc qui s'accordent avec la douce brise marine.

L'éclairage a été un autre élément esthétique clé : les lampes industrielles mélangées au rotin et autres lampes en papier créent une atmosphère chaleureuse qui, associée au bois, crée un esprit de pure détente de vacances. Les meubles caractéristiques ont été fabriqués par des artisans locaux à l'aide de matériaux réutilisés, ou simplement personnalisés pour le projet.

El diseño de esta casa de obra nueva en la Costa Brava responde al requerimiento de una familia que buscaba una casa de campo y de playa a la vez, que les hiciera desconectar del ritmo acelerado de la vida moderna. La arquitectura contemporánea de la construcción del arquitecto Damián Ribas fue el lienzo sobre el que Clara Joly d'Aussy se planteó dotar a la casa de calidez llevando el Mediterráneo y el verde del Empordá, hacia el interior.

Para ello se valió de la madera en muebles y revestimientos, fibras naturales como el ratán, yute y esparto y los tonos beige y tierra. Uno de los mayores desafíos fue separar la cocina, el comedor y el salón. Para tamizar la luz y dividir estos espacios sin cerrarlos, la interiorista utilizó puertas correderas de lamas de madera, en vertical. Las mismas lamas, pero en horizontal, completan armarios y puertas interiores dándole a la casa una continuidad. El porche quedó completamente integrado con el interior gracias a una pérgola de metal y cañizo, y las cortinas de tejido blanco que se acompasan con la suave brisa marina.

La iluminación ha sido otro elemento estético clave: lámparas industriales mezcladas con ratán, y otras de papel, generan un ambiente cálido que combinado con la madera consiguen un espíritu de puro relax vacacional. Los muebles de autor fueron confeccionados por artesanos locales con materiales reutilizados, o sencillamente modificados a medida para el proyecto.

FAR STUDIO

BRITTANY HAKIMFAR - BENJAMIN HAKIMFAR

Far Studio is dedicated to interior design in an organic modernist vein. Based in Philadelphia, but available internationally, the firm creates spaces where comfort and beauty reign. They describe their style as "West Coast design with an East Coast sensibility and a European twist". Brittany Hakimfar is the founder. After graduating from George Washington University with a degree in interior design, she began her career in New York working for Mark Cunningham. In 2012 she moved to Los Angeles to collaborate with renowned designer Waldo Fernandez, where she honed her skills in high-end residential and commercial design. She returned to Philadelphia to start her own design firm with her husband, Benjamin Hakimfar.

Far Studio widmet sich der Innenarchitektur im Stil der organischen Moderne. Das Unternehmen mit Sitz in Philadelphia, das aber auch international tätig ist, schafft Räume, in denen Komfort und Schönheit herrschen. Sie beschreiben ihren Stil als „Westküsten-Design mit einer Ostküsten-Sensibilität und einem europäischen Touch". Brittany Hakimfar ist die Gründerin. Nach ihrem Abschluss in Innenarchitektur an der George Washington University begann sie ihre Karriere in New York, wo sie für Mark Cunningham arbeitete. Im Jahr 2012 zog sie nach Los Angeles, um mit dem renommierten Designer Waldo Fernandez zusammenzuarbeiten, wo sie ihre Fähigkeiten im Bereich hochwertiges Wohn- und Geschäftsdesign verfeinerte. Sie kehrte nach Philadelphia zurück und gründete zusammen mit ihrem Mann Benjamin Hakimfar ihr eigenes Designbüro.

Far Studio se consacre à la décoration intérieure dans une veine moderniste et organique. Basé à Philadelphie, mais disponible à l'international, le cabinet crée des espaces où règnent confort et beauté. Ils décrivent leur style comme « un design de la côte ouest avec une sensibilité de la côte est et une touche européenne ». Brittany Hakimfar est la fondatrice. Après avoir obtenu un diplôme d'architecte d'intérieur à l'université George Washington, elle a commencé sa carrière à New York en travaillant pour Mark Cunningham. En 2012, elle s'est installée à Los Angeles pour collaborer avec le célèbre designer Waldo Fernandez, où elle a affiné ses compétences en matière de design résidentiel et commercial haut de gamme. Elle est retournée à Philadelphie pour créer sa propre agence de design avec son mari, Benjamin Hakimfar.

Far Studio se dedica al diseño de interiores en una vertiente modernista orgánica. Con sede en Filadelfia, pero disponible a nivel internacional, la firma crea espacios en los que impera la comodidad y la belleza. Describen a su estilo como «diseño de la Costa Oeste con una sensibilidad de la Costa Este y un toque europeo». Brittany Hakimfar es la fundadora. Después de graduarse en la Universidad George Washington en diseño de interiores, comenzó su carrera en Nueva York trabajando para Mark Cunningham. En 2012 se trasladó a Los Ángeles para colaborar con el reconocido diseñador Waldo Fernández, donde perfeccionó sus habilidades en el diseño residencial y comercial de alta gama. Regresó a Filadelfia para comenzar su propia empresa de diseño con su marido, Benjamin Hakimfar.

LAKE SHORE PLACE

PALM BEACH, FLORIDA, UNITED STATES

Photos. © Brian Wetzel | Stylist: Kristi Hunter

The owners bought this house during the Covid pandemic, when they decided to replace the frenetic pace of New York City with the slow life of Palm Beach. Given the area's hot climate, the house had to be light and breezy, but also cosy. "They didn't want their house to look cold or austere, or like a holiday spot in Florida," explains Brittany Hakimfar, "that's why they were attracted to my interiors," adds the Far Sudio designer.

Consequently, the aim was to create a space that was both timeless and eclectic. To achieve this, she resorted to neutral tones and the play of different textures with tone-on-tone. Broken whites, bone, and variations of sand, combined with pastels in the children's rooms, created a visual unity throughout much of the house. Natural stone and white oak finishes were also used. The exception was the study with anthracite grey walls that call for introspection.

The studio designed all the bespoke joinery to make the most of the space and created large display windows to showcase ceramics and artwork.

Les propriétaires ont acheté cette maison pendant la pandémie de Covid, lorsqu'ils ont décidé de remplacer le rythme frénétique de New York par la vie lente de Palm Beach. Compte tenu du climat chaud de la région, la maison devait être légère et fraîche, mais aussi confortable. « Ils ne voulaient pas que leur maison ait l'air froide ou austère, ou qu'elle ressemble à un lieu de vacances en Floride », explique Brittany Hakimfar, « c'est pourquoi ils ont été attirés par mes intérieurs », ajoute la designer de Far Sudio.

L'objectif était donc de créer un espace à la fois intemporel et éclectique. Pour y parvenir, elle a recouru à des tons neutres et au jeu des différentes textures en ton sur ton. Des blancs cassés, des os et des variations de sable, associés à des pastels dans les chambres d'enfants, ont créé une unité visuelle dans une grande partie de la maison. Des finitions en pierre naturelle et en chêne blanc ont également été utilisées. L'exception était le bureau aux murs gris anthracite qui appellent à l'introspection.

Le studio a conçu toute la menuiserie sur mesure pour tirer le meilleur parti de l'espace et a créé de grandes fenêtres pour exposer les céramiques et les œuvres d'art.

Die Eigentümer kauften dieses Haus während der Covid-Pandemie, als sie beschlossen, das hektische Tempo von New York City durch das langsame Leben in Palm Beach zu ersetzen. In Anbetracht des heißen Klimas in der Region musste das Haus leicht und luftig, aber auch gemütlich sein. „Sie wollten nicht, dass ihr Haus kalt oder streng aussieht oder wie ein Urlaubsort in Florida", erklärt Brittany Hakimfar, „deshalb fühlten sie sich zu meiner Inneneinrichtung hingezogen", fügt die Far Sudio-Designerin hinzu.

Das Ziel war also, einen Raum zu schaffen, der sowohl zeitlos als auch eklektisch ist. Um dies zu erreichen, griff sie auf neutrale Töne und das Spiel verschiedener Texturen mit Ton-in-Ton zurück. Gebrochenes Weiß, Knochen und Variationen von Sand, kombiniert mit Pastellfarben in den Kinderzimmern, schufen eine visuelle Einheit im gesamten Haus. Auch Naturstein und Weißeiche kamen zum Einsatz. Die Ausnahme war das Arbeitszimmer mit anthrazitgrauen Wänden, die zur Selbstbeobachtung einladen.

Das Studio entwarf alle maßgefertigten Tischlerarbeiten, um den Raum optimal zu nutzen, und gestaltete große Schaufenster zur Präsentation von Keramik und Kunstwerken.

Los propietarios compraron esta casa durante la pandemia del Covid, cuando decidieron sustituir el ritmo frenético de la ciudad de Nueva York por el *slow life* de Palm Beach. En atención al clima caluroso de la zona, la casa debía tener un carácter ligero y fresco, pero también acogedor. «No querían que se su casa se viera fría o austera, o como un sitio para las vacaciones en Florida —explica Brittany Hakimfar— por eso se sintieron atraídos por mis interiores», añade la diseñadora de Far Sudio.

El objetivo fue crear un espacio atemporal y ecléctico a la vez. Para ello recurrió a los tonos neutros y al juego de diferentes texturas con tono sobre tono. Blancos rotos, hueso, y variaciones de arena, combinados con pasteles en las habitaciones infantiles, generaron una unidad visual en gran parte de la vivienda. También utilizó acabados en piedra natural y roble blanco. La excepción fue el estudio con paredes en gris antracita que llaman a la introspección.

El estudió diseñó toda la carpintería a medida con lo que aprovechó al máximo los espacios para generar amplios escaparates y exhibir piezas de cerámica y obras de arte de los propietarios.

GOLANY ARCHITECTS

YARON GOLANY - GALIT GOLANY

Golany Architects is an award-winning design practice based in Tel Aviv. Its principals are the husband and wife team, Yaron Golany and Galit Golany. Their projects are characterized by a strong response to the context, with its cultural and environmental aspects. This results in work that is varied in its formal and material qualities. The projects also vary in size and program, from a 45 m^2 residence to a 45,000 m^2 high-tech campus, and include office buildings, residencial buildings, public buildings, landscape and urban design.

Golany Architects ist ein preisgekröntes Designbüro in Tel Aviv, das von dem Ehepaar Yaron Golany und Galit Golany geleitet wird. Ihre Projekte zeichnen sich durch eine starke Reaktion auf den Kontext, seine kulturellen und ökologischen Aspekte aus. Das Ergebnis sind Arbeiten, die in ihren formalen und materiellen Qualitäten vielfältig sind. Die Projekte sind von unterschiedlicher Größe und Programmatik, von einem 45 m^2 großen Wohnhaus bis zu einem 45 000 m^2 großen High-Tech-Campus, und umfassen Büro-, Wohn-, öffentliche, Landschafts- und Stadtplanungsprojekte.

Golany Architects est un studio de design primé de Tel Aviv, dirigé par l'équipe mari et femme Yaron Golany et Galit Golany. Leurs projets se caractérisent par une forte réaction au contexte, à ses aspects culturels et environnementaux. Le résultat est un travail varié dans ses qualités formelles et matérielles. Les projets sont également variés en termes de taille et de programme, allant d'une résidence de 45 m^2 à un campus high-tech de 45 000 m^2, et comprennent des immeubles de bureaux, des projets résidentiels, publics, paysagers et d'aménagement urbain.

Golany Architects es un galardonado estudio de diseño de Tel Aviv, dirigido por el matrimonio formado por Yaron Golany y Galit Golany. Sus proyectos se caracterizan por una fuerte respuesta al contexto, sus aspectos culturales y medioambientales. El resultado es un trabajo variado en sus cualidades formales y materiales. Los proyectos también son diversos en tamaño y programa, desde una residencia de 45 m^2 a un campus de alta tecnología de 45.000 m^2, e incluyen edificios de oficinas, residenciales, públicos, proyectos paisajísticos y de diseño urbano.

RESIDENCE IN THE GALILEE

GALILEE, ISRAEL

Photos: © Amit Geron, Golany Architects

The house overlooks the Sea of Galilee with a sweeping view from every room. The generous openings, facing the view to the south and east, required shading and filtering against the intense sun provided by the wooden shutters. The shutters can slide in adjustment to the position of the sun, and privacy requirements.

Sustainability and environmental considerations played a key role in the design of the house. To improve climate control, the windows and doors were recessed behind the wooden shutters, creating intermediate spaces, kind of outdoor rooms, which allow for sitting in the fresh country air while preserving privacy and intimacy of indoors. The design helps keeping the house cool and pleasant even during the hottest days of summer.

The house was designed to blend into its pastoral environment. The rugged terrain and the surrounding olive and carob groves, where horses graze, have led to the choice of the house finishes, matching colours and materials for the cement-textured plaster and wooden shutters on the exterior, and light brown stone for the interior flooring and wooden ceiling.

La maison donne sur la mer de Galilée depuis chaque pièce. Les ouvertures généreuses, orientées au sud et à l'est, nécessitaient une protection et une filtration contre le soleil intense grâce à des volets en bois qui peuvent coulisser pour s'adapter à la position du soleil et aux besoins d'intimité.

La durabilité et les considérations environnementales ont joué un rôle clé dans la conception de la maison. Pour améliorer la régulation du climat, les fenêtres et les portes ont été encastrées derrière les volets en bois, créant ainsi des espaces intermédiaires, des sortes de chambres à ciel ouvert, qui permettent de s'asseoir à l'air frais de la campagne tout en préservant l'intimité et la vie privée de l'intérieur. Cette conception permet de garder la maison fraîche et agréable même pendant les journées d'été les plus chaudes.

La maison a été conçue pour se fondre dans son environnement bucolique. Le terrain vallonné et les oliveraies et caroubiers environnants, où paissent les chevaux, ont conduit au choix des finitions de la maison, des couleurs et matériaux assortis pour le plâtre à texture ciment et les volets en bois à l'extérieur, et de la pierre brun clair pour le sol intérieur et le plafond en bois.

Das Haus bietet von jedem Zimmer aus einen Blick auf den See Genezareth. Die großzügigen, nach Süden und Osten ausgerichteten Öffnungen erforderten eine Beschattung und Filterung gegen die intensive Sonne durch hölzerne Fensterläden, die sich je nach Sonnenstand und Sichtschutzbedarf verschieben lassen.

Nachhaltigkeit und Umweltaspekte spielten bei der Gestaltung des Hauses eine wichtige Rolle. Um die Klimatisierung zu verbessern, wurden Fenster und Türen hinter den hölzernen Fensterläden versenkt. So entstanden Zwischenräume, eine Art Freiluftzimmer, in denen man sich an der frischen Landluft aufhalten kann, ohne die Intimität und Privatsphäre des Innenraums zu verlieren. Die Konstruktion trägt dazu bei, dass das Haus auch an den heißesten Sommertagen kühl und angenehm bleibt.

Das Haus wurde so entworfen, dass es sich in seine ländliche Umgebung einfügt. Das hügelige Gelände und die umliegenden Olivenhaine und Johannisbrotbäume, auf denen die Pferde weiden, haben zur Wahl der Oberflächen des Hauses geführt: passende Farben und Materialien für den Zementputz und die hölzernen Fensterläden an der Außenseite und hellbrauner Stein für den Innenboden und die Holzdecke.

La casa tiene vistas al mar de Galilea desde todas las habitaciones. Las generosas aberturas, orientadas al sur y al este, requerían sombra y filtración contra el intenso sol gracias a las contraventanas de madera que pueden deslizarse para adaptarse a la posición del sol y a las necesidades de privacidad.

La sostenibilidad y las consideraciones medioambientales desempeñaron un papel clave en el diseño de la vivienda. Para mejorar el control climático, las ventanas y puertas se empotraron detrás de las contraventanas de madera, creando espacios intermedios, una especie de habitaciones al aire libre, que permiten sentarse al aire fresco del campo preservando la intimidad y privacidad del interior. El diseño ayuda a mantener la casa fresca y agradable incluso durante los días más calurosos del verano.

La casa se diseñó para integrarse en su entorno bucólico. El terreno accidentado y los olivares y algarrobos circundantes, donde pastan los caballos, han propiciado la elección de los acabados de la casa, colores y materiales a juego para el enlucido con textura de cemento y las contraventanas de madera del exterior, y piedra marrón claro para el suelo interior y el techo de madera.

East elevation

South elevation

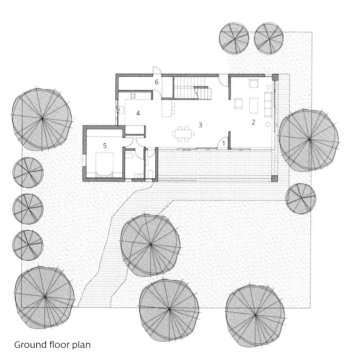

Ground floor plan

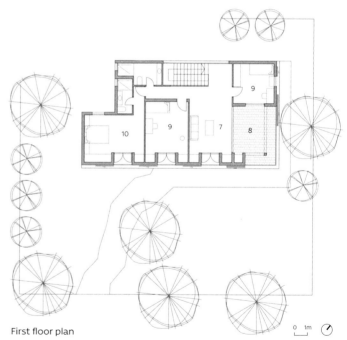

First floor plan

1. Main entrance	6. Pantry
2. Living room	7. Family room
3. Dining room	8. Open balcony
4. Kitchen	9. Bedroom
5. Guest room	10. Master bedroom

I IN

YOHEI TERUI - HIROMU YUYAMA

I IN Inc. is a Tokyo-based design studio founded in 2018 by Yohei Terui and Hiromu Yuyama. The firm is focused on finding innovative solutions in the design of spaces, and proposes striking and surprising interiors. Yohei graduated in Interior Design from Parsons School of Design in New York, after attending Meiji University in Tokyo. Between 2009 and 2017, he worked at Curiosity as a senior designer and before that at New York-based Gabellini Sheppard and SHoP Architects. Hiromu studied architecture and interior design at ICS College of Arts, graduated from Tokyo Gakugei University and worked at Curiosity as a senior designer. Previously, he worked at ILYA in Tokyo.

I IN Inc. ist ein Designstudio mit Sitz in Tokio, das 2018 von Yohei Terui und Hiromu Yuyama gegründet wurde. Das Unternehmen konzentriert sich auf die Suche nach innovativen Lösungen für die Gestaltung von Räumen und schlägt auffallende und überraschende Innenräume vor. Yohei machte seinen Abschluss in Innenarchitektur an der Parsons School of Design in New York, nachdem er die Meiji University in Tokio besucht hatte. Zwischen 2009 und 2017 arbeitete er als Senior Designer bei Curiosity und davor bei Gabellini Sheppard und SHoP Architects in New York. Hiromu studierte Architektur und Innenarchitektur am ICS College of Arts, machte seinen Abschluss an der Tokyo Gakugei University und arbeitete bei Curiosity als Senior Designer. Zuvor arbeitete er bei ILYA in Tokio.

I IN Inc. est un studio de design basé à Tokyo, fondé en 2018 par Yohei Terui et Hiromu Yuyama. Le cabinet s'attache à trouver des solutions innovantes dans la conception des espaces, et propose des intérieurs saisissants et surprenants. Yohei est diplômé en design d'intérieur de la Parsons School of Design de New York, après avoir fréquenté l'université Meiji de Tokyo. Entre 2009 et 2017, il a travaillé chez Curiosity en tant que concepteur principal et, avant cela, chez Gabellini Sheppard et SHoP Architects, basés à New York. Hiromu a étudié l'architecture et la décoration d'intérieur à l'ICS College of Arts, a obtenu un diplôme de l'université Tokyo Gakugei et a travaillé chez Curiosity en tant que designer principal. Auparavant, il a travaillé chez ILYA à Tokyo.

I IN Inc. es un estudio de diseño con sede en Tokio fundado en 2018 por Yohei Terui y Hiromu Yuyama. La firma se orienta a la búsqueda de soluciones innovadoras en el diseño de espacios, y propone interiores impactantes y sorprendentes. Yohei se licenció en Diseño de Interiores en la Parsons School of Design de Nueva York, tras pasar por la Universidad Meiji de Tokio. Entre 2009 y 2017, trabajó en Curiosity como diseñador principal y antes trabajó en las empresas neoyorquinas Gabellini Sheppard y SHoP Architects. Hiromu por su parte, estudió arquitectura y diseño de interiores en el ICS College of Arts. También se graduó en la Universidad Gakugei de Tokio y trabajó en Curiosity como diseñador principal. Anteriormente, trabajó en ILYA en Tokio.

THELIFE SHIBUYA

TOKYO, JAPAN

Photos: © Norihito Yamauchi

I IN was commissioned to give a new life to this 40-year-old flat, under the THELIFE concept of the Good Life real estate group. With an aesthetic that calls for calm and essentials, the Japanese firm proposes a new way of living with a sense of sophistication and luxury.

As soon as you walk through the front door, an abstract volume of natural light welcomes you and reveals space after space, different layers of experiences. In the foyer, a floral piece unfolds above the door, and a solid wood bench taken from a single cherry tree, stands in the warm light.

The predominant tone is pale oak combined with lead grey fittings for a light aesthetic. Wavy glass panels replicate daylight from the bathroom to the entrance. White walls and ceilings highlight the edges of the softly rounded furniture in a nod to the wooden pillars of Japanese temple architecture. The rooms are connected from a minimalist open plan layout. The lines are clean with handle-free doors and furniture, and lighting is concealed in the walls or above the windows. At night, indirect lighting surrounds the entire room.

I IN a été chargé d'insuffler une nouvelle vie à cet appartement vieux de 40 ans dans le cadre du concept THELIFE du groupe immobilier Good Life. Avec une esthétique qui appelle au calme et à l'essentiel, la firme japonaise propose une nouvelle façon de vivre avec un sens de la sophistication et du luxe.

Dès que vous franchissez la porte d'entrée, un volume abstrait de lumière naturelle vous accueille et vous révèle espace après espace, différentes couches d'expériences. Dans le foyer, une pièce florale se déploie au-dessus de la porte, et un banc en bois massif provenant d'un seul cerisier se dresse dans la lumière chaude.

Le ton prédominant est le chêne clair combiné à des accessoires gris plomb pour une esthétique légère. Des panneaux de verre ondulés reproduisent la lumière du jour de la salle de bains à l'entrée. Les murs et les plafonds blancs soulignent les bords des meubles doucement arrondis, en clin d'œil aux piliers en bois de l'architecture des temples japonais. Les chambres sont reliées entre elles par un plan ouvert minimaliste. Les lignes sont épurées, avec des portes et des meubles sans poignée, et l'éclairage est dissimulé dans les murs ou au-dessus des fenêtres. La nuit, un éclairage indirect entoure l'ensemble de la pièce.

I IN wurde beauftragt, dieser 40 Jahre alten Wohnung im Rahmen des THELIFE-Konzepts der Immobiliengruppe Good Life neues Leben einzuhauchen. Mit einer Ästhetik, die nach Ruhe und Wesentlichkeit ruft, schlägt das japanische Unternehmen eine neue Art des Wohnens mit einem Gefühl von Raffinesse und Luxus vor.

Sobald man durch die Eingangstür tritt, empfängt einen ein abstraktes Volumen aus natürlichem Licht und offenbart einen Raum nach dem anderen, verschiedene Schichten von Erfahrungen. Im Foyer entfaltet sich ein Blumenschmuck über der Tür, und eine Massivholzbank, die von einem einzelnen Kirschbaum stammt, steht im warmen Licht.

Der vorherrschende Farbton ist helle Eiche in Kombination mit bleigrauen Beschlägen für eine leichte Ästhetik. Gewellte Glaspaneele lassen das Tageslicht vom Bad in die Küche fallen. Weiße Wände und Decken betonen die Kanten der sanft gerundeten Möbel in Anlehnung an die Holzsäulen der japanischen Tempelarchitektur. Die Zimmer sind durch einen minimalistischen, offenen Grundriss miteinander verbunden. Die Linienführung ist klar, Türen und Möbel sind grifflos, und die Beleuchtung ist in den Wänden oder über den Fenstern versteckt. Nachts umgibt eine indirekte Beleuchtung den gesamten Raum.

I IN se encargó de dar una nueva vida a este piso de 40 años de antigüedad, bajo el concepto de THELIFE del grupo inmobiliario Good Life. Con una estética que llama a la calma y a lo esencial, la firma japonesa propone una nueva forma de vivir con una sensación de sofisticación y lujo.

Apenas se atraviesa la puerta principal, un volumen abstracto de luz natural da la bienvenida y revela espacio tras espacio, diferentes capas de experiencias. En el vestíbulo, una pieza floral se despliega sobre la puerta, y un banco de madera maciza extraída de un solo cerezo, se alza bajo la cálida luz.

El tono predominante es el roble pálido que se combina con accesorios de color gris plomo para lograr una estética ligera. Los paneles de vidrio ondulado replican la luz del día desde el cuarto de baño a la entrada. Las paredes y los techos de color blanco resaltan los bordes de los muebles suavemente redondeados en un guiño a los pilares de madera de la arquitectura de los templos japoneses. Las habitaciones se conectan a partir de un esquema minimalista de planta abierta. Las líneas son limpias con puertas y muebles sin tiradores, y la iluminación está oculta en las paredes o sobre las ventanas. Por la noche, la iluminación indirecta rodea toda la estancia.

JESSICA BATAILLE - THE LIFESTYLE COMPANY

JESSICA BATAILLE

The Jessica Bataille firm was born from the shop – Rust&Co – that the designer established in 1996, when she was 20. At that time, she was a pioneer in transforming Mexican-style furniture with great success. After 25 years, the company has nine companies and more than 60 professionals in architecture, art, design, and engineering. At Jessica Bataille, respect for the environment and sustainability are hallmarks, translated into the Passivhaus. This greenhouse standard aims to create highly energy-efficient homes using advanced insulation and air-sealing techniques. The firm is a Mediterranean reference in architecture and design and promotes the Jávea lifestyle, local craftsmanship, and culture. Also, developing projects in the metaverse and hybrid reality.

Das Unternehmen Jessica Bataille ist aus dem Geschäft Rust&Co- hervorgegangen, das die Designerin 1996 im Alter von 20 Jahren gründete. Zu dieser Zeit war sie eine Pionierin im Transformieren von Möbeln im me- xikanischen Stil, und das mit großem Erfolg. Nach 25 Jahren zählt das Unternehmen neun Unternehmen und mehr als 60 Fachleute in den Bereichen Architektur, Kunst, Design und Technik. Bei Jessica Bataille sind Respekt vor der Umwelt und Nachhaltigkeit Markenzeichen, die sich im Passivhaus widerspiegeln, ein Green-Building-Standard, der darauf abzielt, hochgradig energieeffiziente Gebäude mit fortschrittlichen Isolierungs- und Luftabdichtungstechniken zu schaffen. Das Unternehmen ist eine mediterrane Referenz nicht nur für Architektur und Design, sondern auch für die Förderung des Lebensstils von Jávea, der lokalen Handwerkskunst und Kultur. Auch Entwicklung von Projekten in der Metaversum- und Hybrid-Realität.

Le Studio Jessica Bataille est née de la boutique – Rust&Co – que la créatrice a créée en 1996, alors qu'elle avait 20 ans. À cette époque, elle était une pionnière dans la transformation de meubles de style mexicain, avec un grand succès. Après 25 ans, l'entreprise compte neuf sociétés et plus de 60 professionnels en architecture, art, design et ingénierie. Chez Jessica Bataille, le respect de l'environnement et l'ecologie sont les maîtres mots, traduits dans la Passivhaus, standard de construction écologique qui vise à créer des maisons très économes en énergie en utilisant des techniques d'isolation et d'étanchéité à l'air avancées. L'entreprise est une référence méditerranéenne non seulement en matière d'architecture et de design, mais aussi dans la promotion du style de vie de Jávea, de l'artisanat local et de la culture. Développant également des projets dans le métavers et la réalité hybride.

La firma Jessica Bataille nace de la tienda —Rust&Co— que la diseñadora estableció en 1996, cuando tenía 20 años. En ese momento fue una pionera en transformar muebles de estilo mexicano, con gran éxito. Tras 25 años, la compañía cuenta con nueve empresas y más de 60 profesionales de la arquitectura, el arte, el diseño y la ingeniería. En Jessica Bataille el respeto por el entorno y la sostenibilidad son sellos de identidad, traducidos en las Passivhaus, un estándar de construcción ecológica que tiene como objetivo crear casas de alta eficiencia energética utilizando técnicas avanzadas de aislamiento y sellado del aire. La firma es una referencia mediterránea no sólo en arquitectura y diseño, sino en la promoción del estilo de vida de Jávea, la artesanía local y la cultura. También desarrollando proyectos en el metaverso y la realidad híbrida.

CASCADA HOUSE

JAVEA, ALICANTE, SPAIN

Photos: © Gonzalo Moreno | Web: villacascada.es | Architect: Borja Donderis Pastor | Builder: Team Tip-Top

The house is a perfect conjunction of modern architectural lines and the organic imperfections of the Mediterranean. Lime patches, rounded edges, and high-tech lighting combine and enhance the beauty of nature from sunrise to sunset.

Inside the house, the feeling is that of being surrounded by open spaces that embrace the warm Mediterranean atmosphere. Despite the high ceilings and the maximalism of the architecture, you never have the impression of being alone. Decorative pieces and furniture from different parts of the world add richness and remind you that traveling through the window is possible.

Stone walls embrace and minimize the impact of the architecture to merge the mountain with the building. Natural light pours into the interior creating environments defined by warm materials and natural textures.

The main pillars of the concept are sustainability and beauty. The house has been designed with the input and support of the inspiring owners, who have been closely involved in every final aesthetic decision. Their savoir-vivre has created a perfect bubble of aesthetics and comfort, with well-being and joy in mind.

Das Haus ist eine perfekte Verbindung von modernen architektonischen Linien und den organischen Unvollkommenheiten des Mittel—meers. Kalkflecken, abgerundete Kanten und Hightech-Beleuchtung sorgen dafür, dass die Schönheit der Natur von Sonnenaufgang bis Sonnenuntergang zur Geltung kommt.

Im Inneren des Hauses hat man das Gefühl, von offenen Räumen umgeben zu sein, die die warme mediterrane Atmosphäre einfangen. Trotz der hohen Decken und des Maximalismus der Architektur hat man nie das Gefühl, allein zu sein. Dekorationsgegenstände und Möbel aus verschiedenen Teilen der Welt bereichern den Raum und erinnern daran, dass eine Reise durch das Fenster möglich ist.

Steinmauern umschließen die Architektur und minimieren deren Auswirkungen, um den Berg mit dem Gebäude zu verschmelzen. Natürliches Licht fällt in die Innenräume und schafft Umgebungen, die von warmen Materialien und natürlichen Texturen geprägt sind.

Die wichtigsten Säulen des Konzepts sind Nachhaltigkeit und Schönheit. Das Haus wurde mit dem Input und der Unterstützung der inspirierenden Besitzer entworfen, die eng in jede endgültige ästhetische Entscheidung eingebunden waren. Ihr Savoir-vivre hat eine perfekte Mischung aus Ästhetik und Komfort geschaffen, in der Wohlbefinden und Freude im Vordergrund stehen.

La maison est une conjonction parfaite entre les lignes architecturales modernes et les imperfections organiques de la Méditerranée. Des taches de chaux, des bords arrondis et un éclairage de haute techno- logie se combinent pour mettre en valeur la beauté de la nature, du lever au coucher du soleil.

À l'intérieur de la maison, le sentiment est celui d'être entouré d'espaces ouverts qui embrassent la chaude atmosphère méditerranéenne. Malgré les hauts plafonds et le maximalisme de l'architecture, vous n'avez jamais l'impression d'être seul. Les pièces décoratives et les meubles provenant de différentes parties du monde ajoutent de la richesse et vous rappellent qu'il est possible de voyager par la fenêtre.

Les murs de pierre embrassent et minimisent l'impact de l'architecture afin de fusionner la montagne avec le bâtiment. La lumière naturelle se déverse dans l'intérieur, créant des environnements définis par des matériaux chaleureux et des textures naturelles.

Les principaux piliers du concept de cette maison sont la durabilité et la beauté. La maison a été conçue avec la participation et le soutien des propriétaires inspirés, qui ont été étroitement impliqués dans chaque décision esthétique finale. Leur savoir-vivre a créé une bulle parfaite d'esthétique et de confort, dans un souci de bien-être et de joie.

La casa es una conjunción perfecta de las líneas arquitectónicas modernas y las imperfecciones orgánicas del Mediterráneo. Las manchas de cal, los bordes redondeados y la iluminación de alta tecnología, se combinan y potencian la belleza de la naturaleza, desde el amanecer hasta el atardecer.

Dentro de la casa, la sensación es la de estar rodeado de espacios abiertos que abrazan el cálido ambiente mediterráneo. A pesar de los altos techos y el maximalismo de la arquitectura, nunca se tiene la impresión de estar solo. Las piezas de decoración y los muebles provenientes de diferentes lugares del mundo aportan riqueza y recuerdan que viajar a través de la ventana es posible.

Los muros de piedra abrazan y minimizan el impacto de la arquitectura para fusionar la montaña con la construcción. La luz natural se cuela en el interior creando ambientes definidos por materiales cálidos y texturas naturales.

Los principales pilares del concepto se esta vivienda son la sostenibilidad y la belleza. La casa ha sido diseñada con el aporte y el apoyo de los inspiradores propietarios, que han estado muy cerca en cada decisión estética final. Su savoir-vivre ha creado una burbuja perfecta de estética y confort, pensando en el bienestar y la alegría.

**MARLENE
ULDSCHMIDT
STUDIO**

marleneuldschmidt.com

MARLENE ULDSCHMIDT STUDIO

MARLENE ULDSCHMIDT

The studio was born in 2005 as a space of the German architect Marlene Uldschmidt dedicated to art. The firm is characterised by rigorous processes that begin with inspiration from the place, the clients and the story it is called upon to tell. The idea is obtained through classic and innovative design, a careful selection of textures and materials, and exceptional craftsmanship to work out the interiors. Each project is treated as something unique that involves the effort to achieve an original result with a clear author's stamp. For this reason, each new work always begins with a blank piece of paper. His aim is to conceive a solid, high quality project and to transmit reliability and confidence to his clients, whose dreams he sculpts from the raw material with diligence and honesty.

Das Studio wurde 2005 als ein der Kunst gewidmeter Raum der deutschen Architektin Marlene Uldschmidt gegründet. Das Büro zeichnet sich durch rigorose Prozesse aus, die mit der Inspiration durch den Ort, die Kunden und die Geschichte, die es zu erzählen hat, beginnen. Die Idee wird durch klassisches und innovatives Design, eine sorgfältige Auswahl von Texturen und Materialien sowie außergewöhnliche Handwerkskunst bei der Realisierung der Innenräume umgesetzt. Jedes Projekt wird als etwas Einzigartiges behandelt, bei dem es darum geht, ein originelles Ergebnis zu erzielen, das eindeutig die Handschrift des Autors trägt. Deshalb beginnt jede neue Arbeit immer mit einem leeren Blatt Papier. Sein Ziel ist es, ein solides, qualitativ hochwertiges Projekt zu konzipieren und seinen Kunden, deren Träume er mit Strenge und Ehrlichkeit aus dem Rohmaterial formt, Zuverlässigkeit und Vertrauen zu vermitteln.

Le studio est né en 2005 comme un espace de l'architecte allemande Marlene Uldschmidt dédié à l'art. Le cabinet se caractérise par des processus rigoureux qui commencent par s'inspirer du lieu, des clients et de l'histoire qu'il est appelé à raconter. Cette idée se concrétise par un design classique et innovant, une sélection minutieuse des textures et des matériaux, et un savoir-faire exceptionnel pour la réalisation des intérieurs. Chaque projet est traité comme quelque chose d'unique qui implique l'effort d'atteindre un résultat original avec une empreinte claire de l'auteur. C'est pourquoi chaque nouvelle œuvre commence toujours par une feuille de papier vierge. Son objectif est de concevoir un projet solide et de qualité et de transmettre fiabilité et confiance à ses clients, dont il sculpte les rêves à partir de la matière première avec rigueur et honnêteté.

El estudio nació en 2005 como un espacio de la arquitecta alemana Marlene Uldschmidt dedicado al arte. La firma se caracteriza por llevar a cabo procesos rigurosos que comienzan con la inspiración a partir del lugar, los clientes y la historia que está llamada a contar. La idea se materializa a través del diseño clásico e innovador, una cuidadosa selección de texturas y materiales, y una artesanía excepcional para realizar los interiores. Cada proyecto se trata como algo único que conlleva el esfuerzo por conseguir un resultado original con un claro sello de autor. Por eso, cada nuevo trabajo comienza siempre con un papel en blanco. Su propósito de concebir un proyecto sólido, de gran calidad, y transmitir fiabilidad y confianza a sus clientes, cuyos sueños esculpe de la materia prima con rigor y honestidad.

CASA DOS MORES

CARVOEIRO, ALGARVE, PORTUGAL

Photos: © Renée Kemps

An exceptional viewpoint on a cliff, with open views of the ocean and the infinite horizon, but sheltered by lush vegetation. This is the enclave in which this house is located: pure serenity, invaded by the scent of the sea and graced by the sound of birds. The house is the closest thing to living in a permanent holiday.

The topography offered the rare opportunity to design a house that defies the distinction between inside and outside thanks to the full-height windows, while maintaining a sense of privacy and exclusive seclusion. The use of wood and glass has minimised the impact that typical Portuguese white walls would have created.

Inside, the bright spaces are defined by bold elements such as the wooden staircases and bespoke furniture of exceptional craftsmanship. Two large skylights have been placed to maximise the feeling of being immersed in nature, a distinctive motif in the architectural narrative of the house. All spaces are large and open, with a few selected decorative elements defining them and adding character, while allowing the quality and texture of the solid wood and glass to play their full part.

Un point de vue exceptionnel sur une falaise, avec des vues ouvertes sur l'océan et l'horizon infini, mais abrité par une végétation luxuriante. Telle est l'enclave dans laquelle se trouve cette maison : une pure sérénité, envahie par le parfum de la mer et gratifiée du son des oiseaux. La maison est ce qui se rapproche le plus d'un séjour de vacances permanent.

La topographie offrait la rare opportunité de concevoir une maison qui défie la distinction entre l'intérieur et l'extérieur grâce aux fenêtres pleine hauteur, tout en maintenant un sentiment d'intimité et d'isolement exclusif. L'utilisation du bois et du verre a minimisé l'impact que les murs blancs typiquement portugais auraient créé.

À l'intérieur, les espaces lumineux sont définis par des éléments audacieux tels que les escaliers en bois et le mobilier sur mesure d'une qualité exceptionnelle. Deux grands puits de lumière ont été placés pour maximiser le sentiment d'être immergé dans la nature, un motif distinctif dans le récit architectural de la maison. Tous les espaces sont vastes et ouverts, et quelques éléments décoratifs choisis les définissent et leur donnent du caractère, tout en laissant la qualité et la texture du bois massif et du verre jouer pleinement leur rôle.

Ein außergewöhnlicher Aussichtspunkt auf einer Klippe, mit freiem Blick auf den Ozean und den unendlichen Horizont, aber geschützt durch üppige Vegetation. Das ist die Enklave, in der sich dieses Haus befindet: pure Ruhe, durchdrungen vom Duft des Meeres und begleitet vom Gesang der Vögel. Das Haus kommt dem Leben in einem permanenten Urlaub am nächsten.

Die Topografie bot die seltene Gelegenheit, ein Haus zu entwerfen, das dank der raumhohen Fenster die Unterscheidung zwischen Innen und Außen aufhebt und gleichzeitig ein Gefühl von Privatsphäre und exklusiver Abgeschiedenheit vermittelt. Durch die Verwendung von Holz und Glas wurde die Wirkung der typisch portugiesischen weißen Wände auf ein Minimum reduziert.

Im Inneren werden die hellen Räume durch kühne Elemente wie die Holztreppen und die maßgefertigten Möbel von außergewöhnlicher Handwerkskunst bestimmt. Zwei große Oberlichter wurden angebracht, um das Gefühl, in die Natur eingetaucht zu sein, zu maximieren - ein charakteristisches Motiv in der architektonischen Erzählung des Hauses. Alle Räume sind groß und offen, mit einigen ausgewählten dekorativen Elementen, die sie definieren und ihnen Charakter verleihen, während die Qualität und Textur des Massivholzes und des Glases ihre volle Wirkung entfalten können.

Un mirador excepcional en un acantilado, con vistas abiertas al océano y al horizonte infinito, pero resguardado por una exuberante vegetación. Este es el enclave en el que se encuentra esta casa: pura serenidad, invadida por el aroma del mar y agraciada por el sonido de los pájaros. La vivienda es lo más parecido a vivir en unas vacaciones permanentes.

La topografía ofreció la oportunidad, no tan común, de diseñar una casa que desafía la distinción entre el interior y el exterior gracias a las ventanas de altura completa, manteniendo al mismo tiempo la sensación de privacidad y aislamiento exclusivo. El uso de la madera y cristal ha minimizado el impacto que habrían creado las típicas paredes blancas portuguesas.

En el interior, los espacios luminosos están definidos por elementos audaces, como las escaleras de madera y el mobiliario hecho a medida de una artesanía excepcional. Se han colocado dos grandes claraboyas para maximizar la sensación de estar inmerso en la naturaleza, un motivo distintivo de la narrativa arquitectónica de la casa. Todos los espacios son amplios y abiertos, con pocos elementos decorativos seleccionados que los definen y aportan carácter, al tiempo que permiten que la calidad y la textura de la madera maciza y el cristal desempeñen plenamente su papel.

Site plan and elevation

NC DESIGN &
ARCHITECTURE

ncda.biz

NC DESIGN & ARCHITECTURE

NELSON CHOW

Nelson Chow is renowned for his designs of residential, commercial and hospitality projects with a soft, tactile and welcoming aesthetic. He studied architecture at the University of Waterloo and tailoring at the Fashion Institute of Technology in New York. He began his career at the renowned AvroKO studio, before moving back to Hong Kong, where he set up NCDA in 2011.

Chow first came to prominence in 2016 when his elegant and sophisticated interior design for Foxglove, won the London Restaurant and Bar Design Award for Best Bar in Asia. Since then, the studio has worked for blue-chip international clients. NCDA takes a holistic approach where everything - from the interior, furniture, lighting and graphic design - is customised to create unique narratives.

Nelson Chow ist bekannt für seine Entwürfe für Wohn-, Geschäfts- und Gaststättenprojekte mit einer weichen, taktilen und einladenden Ästhetik. Er studierte Architektur an der University of Waterloo und Schneiderei am Fashion Institute of Technology in New York. Er begann seine Karriere im renommierten Studio AvroKO, bevor er nach Hongkong zurückkehrte, wo er 2011 NCDA gründete.

Chow wurde erstmals 2016 bekannt, als sein elegantes und anspruchsvolles Innendesign für das Foxglove mit dem London Restaurant and Bar Design Award für die beste Bar in Asien ausgezeichnet wurde. Seitdem hat das Studio für erstklassige internationale Kunden gearbeitet. NCDA verfolgt einen ganzheitlichen Ansatz, bei dem alles - von der Inneneinrichtung über die Möbel und die Beleuchtung bis hin zum Grafikdesign - individuell gestaltet wird, um einzigartige Geschichten zu schaffen.

Nelson Chow est réputé pour ses conceptions de projets résidentiels, commerciaux et d'accueil à l'esthétique douce, tactile et accueillante. Il a étudié l'architecture à l'université de Waterloo et la couture au Fashion Institute of Technology de New York. Il a commencé sa carrière au célèbre studio AvroKO, avant de revenir à Hong Kong, où il a créé NCDA en 2011.

Chow s'est fait connaître pour la première fois en 2016 lorsque sa décoration intérieure élégante et sophistiquée pour Foxglove, a remporté le London Restaurant and Bar Design Award du meilleur bar en Asie. Depuis lors, le studio a travaillé pour des clients internationaux de premier ordre. NCDA adopte une approche holistique où tout - de l'intérieur, du mobilier, de l'éclairage et du design graphique - est personnalisé pour créer des récits uniques.

Nelson Chow es famoso por sus diseños de proyectos residenciales, comerciales y de hostelería, con una estética suave, táctil y acogedora. Estudió arquitectura en la Universidad de Waterloo, y sastrería en el Fashion Institute of Technology de Nueva York. Comenzó su carrera en el renombrado estudio AvroKO, antes de trasladarse de nuevo a Hong Kong, donde creó NCDA en 2011.

Chow se dio a conocer en 2016 cuando su elegante y sofisticado interiorismo para Foxglove, ganó el Premio de Diseño de Restaurantes y Bares de Londres como mejor bar de Asia. Desde entonces, el estudio ha trabajado para clientes internacionales de primer orden. NCDA tiene un enfoque holístico donde todo —desde el interior, el mobiliario, la iluminación y el diseño gráfico— se personaliza para crear narrativas únicas.

THE IMPERFECT RESIDENCE

HONG KONG

Photos: © Harold De Puymorin

Nelson Chow was commissioned to design a new home in Hong Kong for some lifelong friends of his. The clients gave him complete freedom with only three conditions: that it be beautiful, functional and age well. Chow came up with a concept with a visually uncluttered design that meets all the conditions. All the elements appear well integrated as part of the architecture and not as separate, scattered objects. On a psychological level, the design relaxes the occupants and feels like an oasis away from the hustle and bustle of Hong Kong. The proposed idea goes beyond the visual and is based on the ancient Japanese philosophy of wabi sabi, which embraces imperfect, impermanent and incomplete beauty. This attitude is the basis of the language that NCDA has translated into a contemporary aesthetic that blends bold geometries with materials in their natural, unfinished state.

The house is divided into three zones. The entrance hall and the living room that resembles a sculpture garden. Here folding panels inspired by Shoji screens conceal the storage units. From there it is on to the bedroom, which emerges on a raised platform and where leather and marble reign supreme. The route ends in the dressing room that merges with the bathroom, providing an uninterrupted and fluid ambience that facilitates relaxation.

Nelson Chow a été chargé de concevoir une nouvelle maison à Hong Kong pour certains de ses amis de longue date. Les clients lui ont donné une liberté totale avec seulement trois conditions : qu'il soit beau, fonctionnel et qu'il vieillisse bien. Chow a proposé un concept au design visuellement épuré qui remplit toutes les conditions. Tous les éléments apparaissent bien intégrés comme faisant partie de l'architecture et non comme des objets séparés et éparpillés. Sur le plan psychologique, le design détend les occupants et leur donne l'impression d'être une oasis loin de l'agitation de Hong Kong.

L'idée proposée va au-delà du visuel et se fonde sur l'ancienne philosophie japonaise du wabi sabi, qui embrasse la beauté imparfaite, impermanente et incomplète. Cette attitude est la base du langage que NCDA a traduit en une esthétique contemporaine qui mêle des géométries audacieuses à des matériaux dans leur état naturel et non fini.

La maison est divisée en trois zones. Le hall d'entrée et le salon qui ressemble à un jardin de sculptures. Ici, des panneaux pliants inspirés des paravents Shoji dissimulent les unités de rangement. De là, on passe à la chambre à coucher, qui émerge sur une plate-forme surélevée et où le cuir et le marbre règnent en maîtres. Le parcours se termine par le dressing qui fusionne avec la salle de bains, offrant une ambiance ininterrompue et fluide qui facilite la relaxation.

Nelson Chow wurde beauftragt, ein neues Haus in Hongkong für einige seiner lebenslangen Freunde zu entwerfen. Die Kunden ließen ihm völlige Freiheit mit nur drei Bedingungen: Es sollte schön und funktionell sein und gut altern. Chow entwickelte ein Konzept mit einem visuell aufgeräumten Design, das alle Bedingungen erfüllt. Alle Elemente erscheinen gut integriert als Teil der Architektur und nicht als separate, verstreute Objekte. Auf psychologischer Ebene entspannt das Design die Bewohner und wirkt wie eine Oase abseits des Trubels in Hongkong.

Die vorgeschlagene Idee geht über das Visuelle hinaus und basiert auf der alten japanischen Philosophie des wabi sabi, die unvollkommene, unbeständige und unvollständige Schönheit anerkennt. Diese Haltung ist die Grundlage für die Sprache, die NCDA in eine zeitgenössische Ästhetik übersetzt hat, die kühne Geometrien mit Materialien in ihrem natürlichen, unbearbeiteten Zustand verbindet.

Das Haus ist in drei Bereiche unterteilt. Die Eingangshalle und das Wohnzimmer, das an einen Skulpturengarten erinnert. Hier verbergen von Shoji-Schirmen inspirierte Faltpaneele die Schränke. Von dort aus geht es weiter zum Schlafzimmer, das auf einem erhöhten Podest liegt und in dem Leder und Marmor die Oberhand haben. Die Reise endet in der Umkleidekabine, die mit dem Badezimmer verschmilzt und eine ununterbrochene und fließende Umgebung bietet, die die Entspannung fördert.

Nelson Chow recibió el encargo de diseñar la nueva casa en Hong Kong de unos amigos suyos de toda la vida. Los clientes le dieron total libertad con sólo tres condiciones: que fuera bonita, funcional y que envejeciera bien. Chow propuso un concepto con ul diseño visualmente despejado y que cumple todas las condiciones. Todos los elementos aparecen bien integrados como parte de la arquitectura y no como objetos separados y dispersos. A nivel psicológico, el diseño relaja a los ocupantes y se siente como un oasis alejado del bullicio de Hong Kong.

La idea propuesta va más allá de lo visual y se basa en la antigua filosofía japonesa del wabi sabi, que abraza la belleza imperfecta, impermanente e incompleta. Esta actitud es la base del lenguaje que NCDA ha traducido en una estética contemporánea que mezcla geometrías atrevidas con materiales en su estado natural inacabado.

La casa se divide en tres zonas. El vestíbulo y la sala de estar que parece un jardín de esculturas. Aquí los paneles plegables inspirados en los biombos Shoji ocultan las unidades de almacenamiento. De allí se pasa al dormitorio que emerge sobre una plataforma elevada y donde impera la piel y el mármol. El trayecto termina en el vestidor que se funde con el cuarto de baño, proporcionando un ambiente ininterrumpido y fluido y facilitando la relajación.

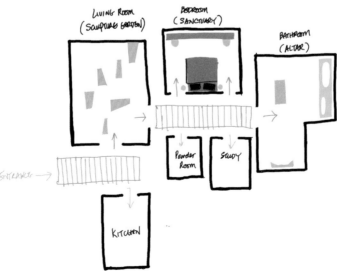

Sketch floor plan

  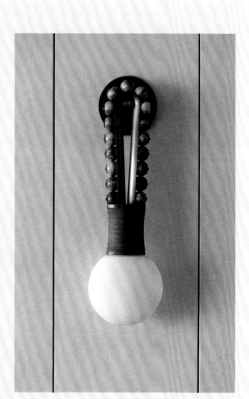

ODELIA BARZILAY INTERIOR DESIGN

ODELIA BARZILAY

Designer, creator, entrepreneur, artist and writer, Odelia Barzilay is the head of the boutique architecture and interior design studio that bears her name. With a career spanning 18 years in the industry, she has worked alongside leading figures in the design and planning of homes of the highest quality standards. Her talent for understanding her clients' needs results in tailor-made projects that make their dreams come true, with professionalism and creativity. The work of the studio is inspired by modern design trends and innovative materials, with a focus on client comfort and quality of life.

Odelia Barzilay, Designerin, Unternehmerin, Künstlerin und Schriftstellerin, ist die Leiterin des Architektur- und Innenarchitekturbüros, das ihren Namen trägt. In ihrer 18-jährigen Karriere in der Branche hat sie mit führenden Persönlichkeiten bei der Gestaltung und Planung von Häusern mit höchsten Qualitätsstandards zusammengearbeitet. Sein Talent, die Bedürfnisse seiner Kunden zu verstehen, führt zu maßgeschneiderten Projekten, die ihre Träume mit Professionalität und Kreativität wahr werden lassen. Ihre Arbeit wird von modernen Designtrends und innovativen Materialien inspiriert, wobei der Komfort und die Lebensqualität der Kunden im Mittelpunkt stehen.

Designer, créatrice, entrepreneuse, artiste et écrivain, Odelia Barzilay est à la tête du studio d'architecture et de décoration intérieure qui porte son nom. Avec une carrière de 18 ans dans le secteur, elle a travaillé aux côtés de personnalités de premier plan dans la conception et la planification de logements répondant aux normes de qualité les plus élevées. Son talent pour comprendre les besoins de ses clients se traduit par des projets sur mesure qui font de leurs rêves une réalité, avec professionnalisme et créativité. Le travail de l'étude s'inspire des tendances du design moderne et des matériaux innovants, en mettant l'accent sur le confort et la qualité de vie des clients.

Diseñadora, creadora, empresaria, artista y escritora, Odelia Barzilay está al frente del estudio boutique de arquitectura y diseño de interiores que lleva su nombre. Con una trayectoria de 18 años en el sector, ha trabajado junto a figuras destacadas del diseño y la planificación de viviendas con los más altos estándares de calidad. Su talento para entender las necesidades de sus clientes, resulta en proyectos a medida que hacen realidad sus sueños, con profesionalidad y creatividad. Su trabajo se inspira en las tendencias del diseño moderno y los materiales innovadores, con un enfoque centrado en la comodidad del cliente y su calidad de vida.

MO HOUSE

HOD HASHARON, ISRAEL

Photos: © Gilad Redt

This house is the result of a complete renovation that brought light and warmth to all the rooms, but above all a sense of calm. The large outdoor garden with fruit trees is accessed through the patio doors adjacent to the main area. The living room is dominated by a combination of wood and metal, which is repeated in the coffee tables and the light fixtures on the ceiling rail. The leather chairs have a wooden frame and the fabric chairs are made of metal. A large central sofa in ecru combines with wool and natural fibre textiles to create an organic look. The parquet floor is of natural oak and has replaced the old one, giving a pleasant homely feel. The dining room and kitchen maintain the same chromatic range, giving priority to textures and matching details such as the hanging lamps.

The suite is located in the attic, which has been divided into different areas to make the most of the space. A glass wall with different degrees of transparency separates the bathroom from the sleeping area. White dominates the furnishings and finishes such as porcelain tiles, interrupted only by the oak floor and the veins of the marble. The bed was covered with materials in the same tonal range to give a relaxed and comfortable feel.

Cette maison est le résultat d'une rénovation complète qui a apporté lumière et chaleur à toutes les pièces, mais surtout un sentiment de calme. Le grand jardin extérieur avec des arbres fruitiers est accessible par les portes-fenêtres adjacentes à la zone principale. Le salon est dominé par une combinaison de bois et de métal, qui se retrouve dans les tables basses et les luminaires du rail de plafond. Les chaises en cuir ont une structure en bois et les chaises en tissu sont en métal. Un grand canapé central en écru se combine avec des textiles en laine et en fibres naturelles pour créer un look organique. Le parquet est en chêne naturel et a remplacé l'ancien, ce qui donne une agréable sensation de confort. La salle à manger et la cuisine conservent la même gamme chromatique, en privilégiant les textures et les détails assortis, comme les lampes suspendues.

La suite est située dans le grenier, qui a été divisé en différentes zones pour tirer le meilleur parti de l'espace. Une paroi en verre avec différents degrés de transparence sépare la salle de bains de la zone de couchage. Le blanc domine l'ameublement et les finitions telles que les carreaux de porcelaine, interrompus seulement par le plancher en chêne et les veines du marbre. Le lit a été recouvert de matériaux de la même gamme de tons pour donner une impression de détente et de confort.

Dieses Haus ist das Ergebnis einer kompletten Renovierung, die allen Räumen Licht und Wärme, vor allem aber ein Gefühl der Ruhe verliehen hat. Der große Garten mit Obstbäumen ist durch die Terrassentüren neben dem Hauptraum zugänglich. Das Wohnzimmer wird von einer Kombination aus Holz und Metall dominiert, die sich in den Couchtischen und den Leuchten an der Deckenschiene wiederfindet. Die Lederstühle haben einen Holzrahmen und die Stoffstühle sind aus Metall. Ein großes zentrales Sofa in Ecru kombiniert mit Textilien aus Wolle und Naturfasern sorgt für einen organischen Look. Der Parkettboden ist aus natürlicher Eiche und hat den alten Fußboden ersetzt, was ein angenehmes Wohngefühl vermittelt. Im Esszimmer und in der Küche wird die gleiche Farbpalette beibehalten, wobei Texturen und passende Details wie die Hängelampen im Vordergrund stehen.

Die Suite befindet sich im Dachgeschoss, das in verschiedene Bereiche unterteilt wurde, um den Raum optimal zu nutzen. Eine Glaswand mit unterschiedlichen Transparenzgraden trennt das Bad vom Schlafbereich. Weiß dominiert das Mobiliar und die Oberflächen, wie z. B. die Porzellanfliesen, die nur durch den Eichenboden und die Maserung des Marmors unterbrochen werden. Das Bett wurde mit Materialien im gleichen Farbtonbereich bezogen, um ein entspanntes und komfortables Gefühl zu vermitteln.

Esta casa es el resultado de una reforma integral que aportó luminosidad y calidez a todos los ambientes, pero sobre todo una sensación de calma. El amplio jardín exterior con árboles frutales se cuela por las puertas del patio adyacente a la zona principal. En el salón predomina una combinación de madera y metal que se repite en las mesas de centro y en los apliques de luz en el riel del techo. Las sillas de cuero tienen estructura de madera, y las de tela, de metal. Un gran sofá central de color crudo, combina con textiles de lana y fibras naturales para crear un aspecto orgánico. El suelo de parquet es de roble natural y ha sustituido al antiguo aportando un agradable aire hogareño. El comedor y la cocina mantienen la misma gama cromática dando prioridad a las texturas y los detalles a juego como las lámparas colgantes.

La suite se encuentra en el ático que se ha dividido en distintas zonas para aprovechar el espacio. Una pared de cristal con distintos grados de transparencia separa el cuarto de baño de la zona de dormitorio. El blanco impera en el mobiliario y los acabados como los azulejos de porcelana, y se interrumpe sólo con el suelo de roble y las vetas del mármol. La cama se cubrió con materiales de la misma gama tonal para dar una sensación relajada y confortable.

Attic plan

Second floor plan

Ground floor plan

STUDIO RAZAVI ARCHITECTURE

ALIREZA RAZAVI

Alireza Razavi (1970) is a registered architect in France, a licensed professional in the USA, and a Chartered Architect in the UK. He holds a Master's Degree from Columbia University in New York and a Master's Degree from the Ecole Nationale des Arts Décoratifs in Paris. Selected as an AD100 Best Designer for 4 consecutive years, his designs cover a wide spectrum or architectural services from interiors to master planning for clients in both the public and private sectors. Operating as one firm with three offices (Paris, New York and London) the studio's portfolio of works spans from Europe to the Americas and includes residential, corporate, hospitality, civic, transportation, and mixed-use projects.

Alireza Razavi (1970) ist in Frankreich und im Vereinigten Königreich als Architekt eingetragen und in den Vereinigten Staaten als Fachmann zugelassen. Er hat einen Master-Abschluss von der Columbia University in New York und einen weiteren von der Ecole Nationale des Arts Décoratifs in Paris. Seine Arbeit, die in vier aufeinander folgenden Jahren als AD100 Best Designer ausgezeichnet wurde, umfasst ein breites Spektrum an architektonischen Dienstleistungen, von Innenräumen bis hin zur Masterplanung. Das Büro verfügt über drei Niederlassungen (Paris, New York und London), und sein Portfolio erstreckt sich von Europa bis nach Amerika mit Projekten in den Bereichen Wohnen, Unternehmen, Gastgewerbe, öffentliche Einrichtungen, Verkehr und Mischnutzung.

Alireza Razavi (1970) est un architecte agréé en France et au Royaume-Uni, et un professionnel agréé aux États-Unis. Il est titulaire d'une maîtrise de l'université Columbia de New York et d'une autre de l'École nationale des arts décoratifs de Paris. Sélectionné comme meilleur designer de l'AD100 pendant quatre années consécutives, son travail couvre un large éventail de services architecturaux, de l'intérieur à la planification générale. Le studio fonctionne comme une entreprise avec trois bureaux (Paris, New York et Londres) et son portefeuille de travaux s'étend de l'Europe à l'Amérique avec des projets résidentiels, d'entreprise, d'hospitalité, civiques, de transport et à usage mixte.

Alireza Razavi (1970) es un arquitecto colegiado en Francia, y el Reino Unido, y profesional autorizado en Estados Unidos. Cuenta con un máster de la Universidad de Columbia en Nueva York, y otro de la Escuela Nacional de Artes Decorativas de París. Seleccionado como mejor diseñador del AD100 durante 4 años consecutivos, sus trabajos abarcan un amplio espectro de servicios arquitectónicos que van desde los interiores hasta la planificación maestra. El estudio opera como una empresa con tres oficinas (París, Nueva York y Londres) y su cartera de trabajos se extiende desde Europa hasta América con proyectos residenciales, corporativos, hospitalarios, cívicos, de transporte y de uso mixto.

APARTMENT XVIII

PARIS, FRANCE

Photos: © Vincent Leroux

This flat overlooking the Luxembourg Gardens is located in a former 18th century mansion that was remodelled in the years after the French Revolution. Since so little of the original features remained and major structural reinforcements had to be made, it was decided to demolish the existing and create a project based on the feelings inspired by the place.

The home is located in one of the oldest areas of Paris (a street registered as a Roman road) and surrounded by a fantastic landscape of private buildings, churches, convents and squares, so architect Alireza Razavi imagined a monastic space. Natural light, which enters from three different directions, has been the main raw material. The quality of the building is expressed in the interior with generous load-bearing walls and columns, further emphasising its materiality with the application of a plaster stucco that rubs against the light. The selection of soft finishes and the abundant use of curved shapes to avoid harsh shadows has created a tranquil space, where sound, light and vision form part of a coherent whole. The design and selection of the furniture, as well as all the artworks in the flat, are part of a single narrative and spatial experience.

Cet appartement, qui donne sur les jardins du Luxembourg, est situé dans un ancien hôtel particulier du XVIIIe siècle, remodelé dans les années qui ont suivi la Révolution française. Comme il ne restait que très peu d'éléments d'origine et que d'importants renforcements structurels devaient être effectués, il a été décidé de démolir l'existant et de créer un projet basé sur les sentiments inspirés par le lieu.

La maison est située dans l'un des plus anciens quartiers de Paris (une rue inscrite comme voie romaine) et entourée d'un paysage fantastique de bâtiments privés, d'églises, de couvents et de places. L'architecte Alireza Razavi a donc imaginé un espace monastique. La lumière naturelle, qui entre par trois directions différentes, a été la principale matière première. La qualité du bâtiment s'exprime à l'intérieur par des murs porteurs et des colonnes généreuses, soulignant encore sa matérialité par l'application d'un stuc plâtreux qui se frotte à la lumière. La sélection de finitions douces et l'utilisation abondante de formes courbes pour éviter les ombres dures ont créé un espace tranquille, où le son, la lumière et la vision font partie d'un tout cohérent. La conception et la sélection du mobilier, ainsi que toutes les œuvres d'art de l'appartement, font partie d'une seule et même expérience narrative et spatiale.

Diese Wohnung mit Blick auf die Luxemburger Gärten befindet sich in einem ehemaligen Herrenhaus aus dem 18. Jahrhundert, das in den Jahren nach der Französischen Revolution umgebaut wurde. Da so wenig von der ursprünglichen Bausubstanz erhalten geblieben war und erhebliche strukturelle Verstärkungen vorgenommen werden mussten, wurde beschlossen, das bestehende Gebäude abzureißen und ein Projekt zu schaffen, das auf den von diesem Ort inspirierten Gefühlen basiert.

Das Haus befindet sich in einem der ältesten Viertel von Paris (eine Straße, die als Römerstraße registriert ist) und ist von einer fantastischen Landschaft mit privaten Gebäuden, Kirchen, Klöstern und Plätzen umgeben, so dass der Architekt Alireza Razavi sich einen klösterlichen Raum vorgestellt hat. Natürliches Licht, das aus drei verschiedenen Richtungen einfällt, war das wichtigste Ausgangsmaterial. Die Qualität des Gebäudes kommt im Inneren mit großzügigen tragenden Wänden und Säulen zum Ausdruck, wobei die Materialität des Gebäudes durch die Verwendung eines Gipsstucks, der sich am Licht reibt, noch betont wird. Durch die Auswahl weicher Oberflächen und die reichliche Verwendung geschwungener Formen zur Vermeidung harter Schatten wurde ein ruhiger Raum geschaffen, in dem Klang, Licht und Sicht ein kohärentes Ganzes bilden. Das Design und die Auswahl der Möbel sowie alle Kunstwerke in der Wohnung sind Teil einer einzigen Erzählung und Raumerfahrung.

Este apartamento con vistas a los jardines de Luxemburgo, se encuentra en una antigua mansión del siglo XVIII remodelada en los años posteriores a la revolución francesa. Puesto que quedaba tan poco de las características originales y había que hacer importantes refuerzos estructurales, se optó por demoler lo existente y crear un proyecto a partir de los sentimientos que inspiraba el lugar.

La vivienda está situada en una de las zonas más antiguas de París (una calle registrada como una vía romana) y rodeada de un fantástico paisaje de edificios privados, iglesias, conventos y plazas, por ello el arquitecto Alireza Razavi imaginó un espacio monástico. La luz natural que entra desde tres direcciones diferentes, ha sido la principal materia prima. La calidad del edificio se expresa en el interior con generosos muros de carga y columnas, resaltando además su materialidad con la aplicación de un estuco de yeso que roza con la luz. La selección de acabados suaves y el uso abundante de las formas curvas para evitar las sombras duras, ha creado un espacio tranquilo, donde el sonido, la luz y la visión forman parte de un todo coherente. El diseño y la selección de los muebles, así como todas las obras de arte del apartamento, forman parte de una única narrativa y experiencia espacial.

STUDIO
STOOKS

studiostooks.com.au

STUDIO STOOKS

ASH STUCKEN
Collaborator: MIRANDA GEIGER

Studio Stooks focuses on connecting nature and architecture through rigorous design that links place and person. Director, Ash Stucken's buildings are intended to be a reflection of their place, time and people and are made with the intention of ageing gracefully. His overall aim is to achieve timelessness in a fast-moving industry and world. Ash Stucken and Miranda Geiger's collaborative work on Karri Loam seeks to celebrate the passage of time and encourage a sense of being present. Tactility is a strong theme that is explored through natural materials and craftsmanship, experimenting with contrasting finishes, from raw and rough, to minimalist and refined.

Das Studio Stooks konzentriert sich auf die Verbindung von Natur und Architektur durch strenges Design, das Ort und Mensch miteinander verbindet. Die Gebäude des Direktors Ash Stucken sollen den Ort, die Zeit und die Menschen widerspiegeln und mit der Absicht gebaut werden, anmutig zu altern. Sein übergeordnetes Ziel ist es, in einer schnelllebigen Industrie und Welt Zeitlosigkeit zu erreichen. Ash Stucken und Miranda Geiger wollen mit ihrer gemeinsamen Arbeit an Karri Loam das Vergehen der Zeit feiern und ein Gefühl der Gegenwärtigkeit fördern. Taktilität ist ein starkes Thema, das durch natürliche Materialien und Handwerkskunst erforscht wird, wobei mit kontrastreichen Oberflächen experimentiert wird, von roh und rau bis hin zu minimalistisch und raffiniert.

Le Studio Stooks s'attache à relier la nature et l'architecture par une conception rigoureuse qui établit un lien entre le lieu et la personne. Les bâtiments du directeur, Ash Stucken, se veulent le reflet de leur lieu, de leur époque et de leurs habitants et sont conçus dans l'intention de vieillir avec élégance. Son objectif global est d'atteindre l'intemporalité dans un secteur et un monde en évolution rapide. Le travail de collaboration d'Ash Stucken et Miranda Geiger sur Karri Loam cherche à célébrer le passage du temps et à encourager le sentiment d'être présent. La tactilité est un thème fort qui est exploré à travers les matériaux naturels et l'artisanat, en expérimentant des finitions contrastées, allant du brut et de la rugosité au minimaliste et au raffiné.

Studio Stooks se centra en conectar la naturaleza y la arquitectura a través de un diseño riguroso que vincula lugar y persona. Los edificios de su director, Ash Stucken, pretenden ser un reflejo de su lugar, su tiempo y su gente, y están hechos con la intención de envejecer con gracia. Su objetivo general es lograr la atemporalidad en un sector y un mundo que evoluciona con rapidez. El trabajo conjunto de Ash Stucken y Miranda Geiger en Karri Loam pretende celebrar el paso del tiempo y fomentar la sensación de estar presente. El tacto es un tema importante que se explora a través de materiales naturales y artesanía, experimentando con acabados contrastados, desde crudos y ásperos hasta minimalistas y refinados.

KARRI LOAM

MARGARET RIVER, AUSTRALIA

Photos: © Glenn Russell & Studio Stooks, Rachel Claire

Conceived as a retreat or short-term rental house, Karri Loam is located in a residential area overlooking the ancient Karri Forest on the Margaret River. The building has two levels that define the design concept through two different experiences. On the ground floor the occupant is immersed in the solidity of the rammed earth walls, but is liberated when, via a wooden staircase, he or she enters the light space of the first floor, facing the treetops.

All excess is deliberately omitted. Clean surfaces, neutral tones and essential, comfortable furnishings reduce visual noise and draw the eye inwards. The materials are inspired by the early country houses built in the 80's with local and accessible materials. The project uses a local mix of lime and eucalyptus sediment for the steady earth walls. The paints are natural lime and the timbers are Australian, many of which were naturally fallen. To enhance the tactile qualities of the materials they worked with local craftsmen who shaped the rough sawn eucalyptus boards, and the highly skilled finish of the micro-cement surfaces.

Conçu comme une retraite ou une maison de location à court terme, Karri Loam est situé dans une zone résidentielle surplombant l'ancienne forêt de Karri sur la Margaret River. Le bâtiment comporte deux niveaux qui définissent le concept de design à travers deux expériences différentes. Au rez-de-chaussée, l'occupant est immergé dans la solidité des murs en terre battue, mais il est libéré lorsque, par un escalier en bois, il pénètre dans l'espace lumineux du premier étage, face à la cime des arbres.

Tout excès est délibérément omis. Des surfaces propres, des tons neutres et un mobilier essentiel et confortable réduisent le bruit visuel et attirent le regard vers l'intérieur. Les matériaux sont inspirés des premières maisons de campagne construites dans les années 80 avec des matériaux locaux et accessibles. Le projet utilise un mélange local de chaux et de sédiment d'eucalyptus pour les murs en terre stabilisée. Les peintures sont à la chaux naturelle et les bois sont australiens, dont beaucoup sont tombés naturellement. Pour améliorer les qualités tactiles des matériaux, ils ont travaillé avec des artisans locaux qui ont façonné les planches d'eucalyptus brutes de sciage, et la finition hautement qualifiée des surfaces en microciment.

Karri Loam wurde als Rückzugsort oder als Haus für Kurzzeitmieten konzipiert und befindet sich in einem Wohngebiet mit Blick auf den alten Karri Forest am Margaret River. Das Gebäude besteht aus zwei Ebenen, die das Designkonzept durch zwei unterschiedliche Erfahrungen definieren. Im Erdgeschoss ist der Bewohner in die Solidität der Stampflehmwände eingetaucht, wird aber befreit, wenn er über eine Holztreppe in den hellen Raum des ersten Stocks mit Blick auf die Baumkronen gelangt.

Auf alles Überflüssige wird bewusst verzichtet. Klare Oberflächen, neutrale Töne und wesentliche, bequeme Einrichtungsgegenstände reduzieren den visuellen Lärm und lenken den Blick nach innen. Die Materialien sind von den frühen Landhäusern inspiriert, die in den 80er Jahren mit lokalen und zugänglichen Materialien gebaut wurden. Das Projekt verwendet eine lokale Mischung aus Kalk und Eukalyptussediment für die festen Lehmwände. Die Farben sind aus natürlichem Kalk und die Hölzer aus Australien, von denen viele natürlich gefallen sind. Um die taktilen Qualitäten der Materialien hervorzuheben, arbeiteten sie mit lokalen Handwerkern zusammen, die die sägerauen Eukalyptusbretter und die hochqualifizierte Oberfläche des Mikrozements formten.

Concebida como una casa para retiros o de alquiler de corta duración, Karri Loam se encuentra en un pueblo mirando hacia el antiguo bosque de Karri, en el río Margaret. La construcción tiene dos niveles que definen el concepto de diseño a través de dos experiencias diferentes. En la planta baja el ocupante está inmerso en la solidez de los muros de tierra apisonada, pero se libera cuando a través de una escalera de madera, se adentra en el espacio ligero orientado hacia las copas de los árboles en la segunda planta.

Todo exceso está omitido a propósito. Superficies limpias, tonos neutros y mobiliario esencial y confortable reducen el ruido visual y llevan la mirada hacia el interior. Los materiales de la obra se inspiran en las casas de campo construidas por sus habitantes con materiales de la zona y accesibles. El proyecto utiliza una mezcla local de cal y sedimento de eucalipto para los muros de tierra estabilizada. Las pinturas son de cal natural y las maderas australianas y principalmente caídas de forma natural. Para realzar las cualidades táctiles de los materiales se trabajó con artesanos locales que dieron forma a las tablas de eucalipto aserradas en bruto, y al acabado altamente cualificado de las superficies de microcemento.

Longitudinal section

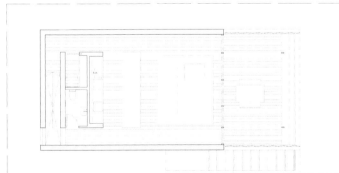

First floor plan

Ground floor plan

ZOZAYA ARQUITECTOS

DANIEL ZOZAYA - ENRIQUE ZOZAYA

Father and son make up this architectural studio linked to the Pacific coast. Enrique Zozaya studied at La Salle University. He worked as a project developer for Ricardo Legorreta and Ramírez Vázquez, which influenced the architecture he developed in the following years in Zihuatanejo, Mexico, where he founded the firm in 1986. His contact with life in the tropics on the coast of Guerrero has allowed him to create his own style, influenced by his daily observation of the climate and nature. Daniel Zozaya, for his part, studied architecture at the Universidad Iberoamericana and his incorporation into the firm in 2015 has involved a leap towards new technologies. He is an expert in creating idyllic private homes that blend the local and the global.

Vater und Sohn bilden dieses Architekturbüro an der Pazifikküste. Enrique Zozaya studierte an der Universität La Salle. Er arbeitete als Projektentwickler für Ricardo Legorreta und Ramírez Vázquez, was die Architektur beeinflusste, die er in den folgenden Jahren in Zihuatanejo, Mexiko, entwickelte, wo er 1986 das Büro gründete. Sein Kontakt mit dem Leben in den Tropen an der Küste von Guerrero hat es ihm ermöglicht, seinen eigenen Stil zu kreieren, der von seinen täglichen Beobachtungen des Klimas und der Natur beeinflusst ist. Daniel Zozaya seinerseits hat an der Universidad Iberoamericana Architektur studiert. Seine Aufnahme in das Büro im Jahr 2015 bedeutete einen Sprung in Richtung neuer Technologien. Er ist Experte für die Gestaltung idyllischer Privathäuser, die das Lokale mit dem Globalen verbinden.

Père et fils composent ce studio d'architecture lié à la côte Pacifique. Enrique Zozaya a étudié à l'université La Salle. Il a travaillé comme développeur de projets pour Ricardo Legorreta et Ramírez Vázquez, ce qui a influencé l'architecture qu'il a développée dans les années suivantes à Zihuatanejo, au Mexique, où il a fondé le cabinet en 1986. Son contact avec la vie sous les tropiques, sur la côte de Guerrero, lui a permis de créer son propre style, influencé par son observation quotidienne du climat et de la nature. Daniel Zozaya, quant à lui, a étudié l'architecture à l'Universidad Iberoamericana et son incorporation au cabinet en 2015 a signifié un saut vers les nouvelles technologies. Il est expert dans la création de résidences privées idylliques qui mêlent le local et le global.

Padre hijo, conforman este estudio de arquitectura ligado a la costa del Pacífico. Enrique Zozaya estudió en la Universidad La Salle. Trabajó como promotor de proyectos para Ricardo Legorreta y Ramírez Vázquez, lo que influyó en la arquitectura que desarrolló en los años siguientes en Zihuatanejo donde fundó el despacho en 1986. Su contacto con la vida del trópico en la costa guerrerense, le ha permitido crear un estilo propio muy influido por la observación cotidiana del clima y la naturaleza. Daniel Zozaya, por su parte, estudió Arquitectura en la Universidad Iberoamericana y su incorporación al despacho en 2015 ha implicado el salto hacia las nuevas tecnologías. Es un experto en la creación de casas privadas idílicas que mezclan lo local y lo global.

CASA DEL ACANTILADO

GUERRERO, MÉXICO

Photos: © Rafael Gamo

Perched on cliffs battered by the force of the sea, this house is located in the bay of Zihuatanejo, on the Pacific coast. Its position is that of a lighthouse that warns fishermen and provides light. Its spirit is that of the rock from which it emerges, mimicking the context and putting into practice the craft techniques and vernacular architecture of the place. In this project the topography is a determining factor in the spatial layout.

The house is entered directly from the upper floor, without an access door. A palapa of stone, wood and palm leaves is made by local labour, welcoming and housing the social area exposed to the cliffs. Its shape takes advantage of natural light and cross ventilation to reduce energy consumption. The staircase leading to the private area is framed by uncovered concrete walls and terminates in a pool contained by walls that frame the infinity continuity with the Pacific. The foyer links to the bedrooms, each with private terraces that open onto spaces for contemplation of the incredible landscape.

Perchée sur des falaises battues par la force de la mer, cette maison est située dans la baie de Zihuatanejo, sur la côte Pacifique. Sa position est celle d'un phare qui avertit les pêcheurs et fournit de la lumière. Son esprit est celui de la roche d'où il émerge, imitant le contexte et mettant en pratique les techniques artisanales et l'architecture vernaculaire du lieu. Dans ce projet, la topographie est un facteur déterminant dans l'organisation spatiale.

On entre directement dans la maison par l'étage supérieur, sans porte d'accès. Une palapa de pierre, de bois et de feuilles de palmier est fabriquée par la main-d'œuvre locale, accueillant et abritant l'espace social exposé aux falaises. Sa forme tire parti de la lumière naturelle et de la ventilation croisée pour réduire la consommation d'énergie. L'escalier menant à la zone privée est encadré par des murs en béton non couverts et se termine par une piscine contenue par des murs qui encadrent la continuité à l'infini avec le Pacifique. Le foyer relie les chambres, chacune avec des terrasses privées qui s'ouvrent sur des espaces de contemplation de l'incroyable paysage.

Dieses Haus liegt in der Bucht von Zihuatanejo an der Pazifikküste auf einer Klippe, die von der Kraft des Meeres umspült wird. Seine Position ist die eines Leuchtturms, der die Fischer warnt und Licht spendet. Der Geist des Felsens, aus dem es entstanden ist, wird durch die Nachahmung des Kontextes und die Umsetzung der handwerklichen Techniken und der volkstümlichen Architektur des Ortes geprägt. Bei diesem Projekt ist die Topographie ein entscheidender Faktor für die räumliche Organisation.

Das Haus wird direkt vom Obergeschoss aus betreten, ohne eine Zugangstür. Ein Palapa aus Stein, Holz und Palmblättern wurde von einheimischen Arbeitern errichtet und beherbergt den sozialen Bereich, der den Klippen ausgesetzt ist. Seine Form nutzt das natürliche Licht und die Querlüftung, um den Energieverbrauch zu senken. Die Treppe, die zum privaten Bereich führt, wird von unverkleideten Betonwänden eingerahmt und endet in einem Pool, der von Mauern umgeben ist, die die unendliche Kontinuität mit dem Pazifik einrahmen. Vom Foyer aus gelangt man zu den Schlafzimmern, die alle über private Terrassen verfügen, von denen aus man die unglaubliche Landschaft betrachten kann.

Postrada sobre acantilados golpeados por la fuerza del mar, se encuentra esta casa, en la bahía de Zihuatanejo, costa del Pacífico. Su posición es la de un faro que avisa a los pescadores y proporciona luz. Su espíritu es el de la roca de la que emerge mimetizándose con el contexto y poniendo en práctica las técnicas artesanales y la arquitectura vernácula del sitio. En este proyecto la topografía es un factor determinante para la organización espacial.

A la casa se entra directamente desde la planta alta y no hay puerta de acceso. Una palapa da la bienvenida y alberga el área social expuesta a los acantilados. La palapa de piedra, madera y hojas de palma, está hecha por mano de obra local. Su forma aprovecha la luz natural y una ventilación cruzada que reduce el consumo de energía. La escalera de acceso a la zona privada está enmarcada por muros de hormigón descubiertos y terminan en una piscina contenida por muros de que enmarcan la continuidad infinita con el Pacífico. El vestíbulo enlaza con las habitaciones, cada una con terrazas privadas que se abren a espacios de contemplación hacia el increíble paisaje.

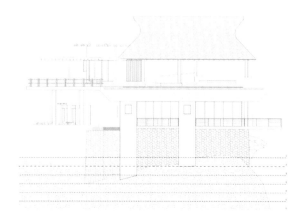

Facade towards the sea

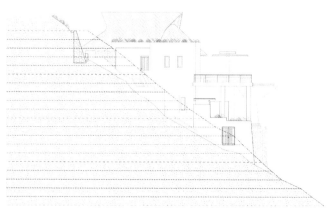

Side façade